WITH RECIPES FROM THE KITCHENS OF
YORKSHIRE'S FAVOURITE ITALIAN RESTAURANT

The Salvo's story

MY FAMILY & OTHER ITALIANS

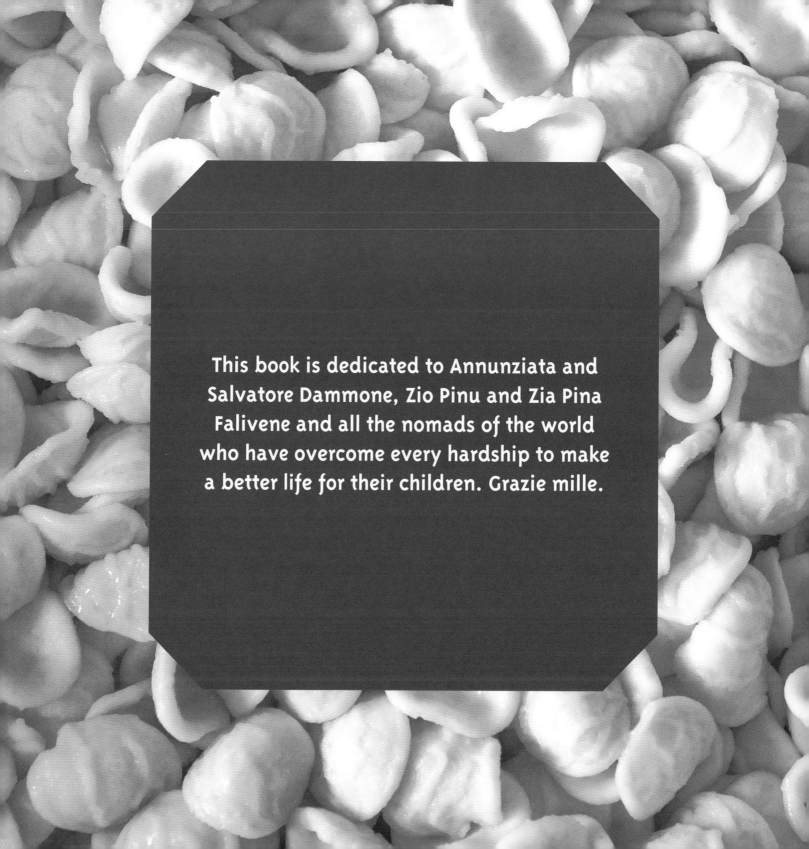

This book is dedicated to Annunziata and Salvatore Dammone, Zio Pinu and Zia Pina Falivene and all the nomads of the world who have overcome every hardship to make a better life for their children. Grazie mille.

Written by:
John and Gip Dammone
with Martin Edwards

Edited by:
Christopher Brierley

Home economist:
Paul Orton

Design by:
Richard Abbey

Photography by:
Tim Green
www.timgreenphotographer.co.uk
Additional photographs supplied by Salvo's
© John and Gip Dammone

First published in 2015 on behalf of:
Salvo's – www.salvos.co.uk
Otley Road, Leeds
Tel: 0113 275 5017

Published by:
RMC Books – www.rmcbooks.co.uk
6 Broadfield Court, Sheffield, S8 0XF
Tel: 0114 250 6300

Salvo's

2011 - John and Gip outside Salvo's

Marks and Spencer, Morecambe and Wise, Mills and Boon. You can't have the one without the other. It just doesn't work.

Likewise me and my brother Gip. We're a duo bonded not only by family ties but by a shared dedication to the very finest Italian food. It's what Salvo's Restaurant is built on.

It's the result of a process which spans six decades and two generations of the same family.

So we're pleased to present a celebration of the good Italian cooking that has been our byword over all those years. This is our story.

Small Plates,
Coffee & Wine.
Served till 10pm
––––––––
Arancini
Meatballs
Pasta
Platters

Salvo's Salumeria

We are open all day until
offering casual dining & drin
feel free to enjoy anything fro
glass of Prosecco with assorted cro
coffee and cake, or pick a few ta
from our Stuzzichi menu and
them with friends.

Wednesday, Thursday & Friday evening
offer our "Cenare con Amici" Supper.
This is true Italian family style
Book your table and enjoy the surpri
what the chef will cook for you.
Dinner is £22.95

Saturday's are home to our...
Regional Dinners.
We serve a tasting menu from one of
chosen regions of Italy. Please a
which region we are currently st
Tables are available to book in ad
for our Cenare con Amici & Regiona
Dinners.

{ origins }

Salvatore Dammone was a handsome guy. And he knew it. Posing for the camera in his Carabinieri uniform, he cuts a dashing figure. The time was the early 1950s, an era when, in common with the rest of Europe, Italy had emerged from post-war austerity and was beginning to enjoy life again.

The suits were sharp, the cars stylish and, just like in the movies, the vita was definitely dolce.

The young Salvatore had, in his boyhood years, shown an early acumen for business, selling cigarettes to the occupying German troops on his home island of Sicily. Never one to miss an opportunity, he was unaffected by the changing fortunes of war and continued his trade, the only difference being that the customers now wore American battledress.

Soon his turn to don a uniform came after joining the Carabinieri, the Italian national police force. In doing so, he made a decision which was to shape the rest of his life, and reveal a destiny in a far-off country.

Salvo, as he became known, found himself posted to the mainland, to the southern Italian city of Salerno. His charm and good looks did not go unnoticed by its female inhabitants, not least 20-year-old Nunzia Calce.

Salvatore Dammone in his Carabinieri uniform

Nunzia Calce — soon to be Dammone — on her Vespa in southern Italy

Romance followed, but there were certain hurdles to be cleared before they could be together. Salvo's mother Agata, making her first trip across the short stretch of sea that divides the mainland and Sicily, arrived to run the rule over her prospective daughter-in-law.

In turn, Salvo came under the scrutiny of Nunzia's mother Francesca, who immediately took a shine to the young Sicilian. His visits to the family home were always marked by fabulous feasts, all cooked up in her broom cupboard-sized kitchen by the lady her grandchildren would come to know as Nonna Francesca.

But maternal approval was one thing. The formidable Italian state police was quite another.

Regulations specifically forbade serving officers to marry someone in the same town they were serving in. Why this should be, we can only guess. But faced with the choice of career or waiting, the 26-year-old Salvo didn't hesitate. The wedding was set for 27th February 1954.

These days, a foreigner seeing an Italian wedding for the first time might well conclude that the event was primarily an occasion for guests to indulge in a marathon eating session, the spectacle of a couple pledging the rest of their lives to each other being something of a sideshow in comparison.

Ten-course (or more) menus are not unusual and the dining experience can last for many hours.

But in the tiny apartment that was the bride's home, there wasn't room to swing a cannelloni.

Every chair in the apartment block was requisitioned from neighbours for the reception. The bill of fare was restricted to plates of small sweet pastries passed around along with glasses of limoncello made by Nunzia's mother. There was just enough room for a table, on which the wedding presents were proudly displayed.

After a short honeymoon in Milan, the happy couple might well have settled in Salerno and built a life together there. But fate had already decreed their future lay elsewhere, in a country of which they knew little.

The suits were sharp, the cars stylish and, just like in the movies, the vita was definitely dolce.

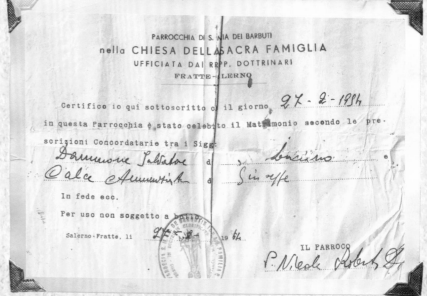

Love and marriage...
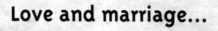

CANNOLI SICILIANI

Pops was from Sicily and, like all Sicilians, he constantly craved returning to the homeland to stock up on the family's home-cured and baked olives and to eat a cannoli or two every day.

These crispy pasta shells are filled with sweetened sheep's ricotta and candied fruit. Chopped chocolate is sometimes added. You will need some metal cannoli tubes – it's easy to find them cheaply online, or you could always saw your broom handle into four-inch pieces.

INGREDIENTS

300g plain flour

30g icing sugar

25g butter

5g good cocoa powder

130g sweet Marsala wine

Pinch salt

1. First make the dough (makes about 30 shells).

2. Sift the flour, rub the butter in and incorporate the rest of the ingredients. Knead until the mixture resembles pasta dough. Cover and rest for 30 minutes.

3. Cut the dough into four and roll out strips in a pasta rolling machine set to three (about 2mm).

4. Use a 90mm ring and cut out the pasta discs. Alternatively, you can use a regular cup to cut out if you are ringless.

5. Wrap around cannoli tubes using a little egg wash to join the ends and deep-fry at 180°C for two minutes. Place on absorbent kitchen paper to cool slightly.

6. Slide the tubes out and repeat.

Continued on the next page...

CANNOLI SICILIANI (CONTINUED)

We are lucky at Salvo's in having a Sardinian fella close by who makes sheep's milk ricotta for us to order using local Yorkshire ewes milk. This allows us to make cannoli to the traditional recipe. Cow's milk ricotta is widely available and, though milder in flavour, still produces a delicious filling. Simply cream the ricotta by whisking, sweeten to your taste and add some chopped candied fruit, cherries and dark chocolate. Don't smash the choc up too much as the filling will become too dark.

For the filling:
700g ricotta
1 shot of white rum
75g dark chocolate
250g icing sugar
150g candied fruit

1. Drain the ricotta well. Add sugar and rum, whip till smooth and creamy. Add candied fruit and fold in chopped chocolate.
2. Use a piping bag to fill the cannoli, then dredge with icing sugar. Garnish the ends with some candied fruit or chocolate and eat within a couple of hours.
3. If you don't want to eat all 30 in one day the shells keep well in a biscuit tin for a week or so.

Chef Guiseppe — cannolis
make him smile!

TORTA ALL'ARANCIA E CIOCCOLATA

Pops was raised in the town of Palagonia, about 30 miles inland from Catania in an area lauded for its citrus fruits, oranges in particular. Whenever our weekly deliveries come in from Milan with oranges on the order, invariably the blood oranges are from Palagonia, which I love.

This orange and chocolate cake is flourless, using ground almonds and polenta and good juicy oranges which result in a very moist cake. It's just delicious served with créme fraîche sweetened with a generous blob of chunky marmalade.

INGREDIENTS

2 wax free oranges
175g ground almonds
75g polenta
250g sugar
5 medium eggs
150g dark chocolate chips
1 teaspoon baking powder

1. Pre-heat the oven to 180°C.
2. Wash and poach the oranges in water until soft for an hour or so and leave to cool. Quarter, remove any pips and purée roughly in a food processor leaving some body in the oranges rather than a smooth purée.
3. Whisk the eggs with the sugar till you get a thick cream texture. Mix in the ground almonds, polenta and baking powder.
4. Mix in the orange pulp and chocolate chips.
5. Pour the cake mix, which is thick but just pourable, into a greased and floured spring-loaded cake tin (line the base with greaseproof paper first).
6. Bake for 45 minutes and remove from tin when cool.
7. To test, push a skewer into the cake – it will come out clean when done.

PESCE 'IN UMIDO'

One of mum's favourite ways to cook fish was *'in umido'* where fillets of cod (or sole, haddock or plaice) are gently stewed in their own juices with a few flavourings. They're then served with lettuce leaves dressed with olive oil and salt and a chunk of fresh bread. Proper Italian fast food, this can be on the table in 15 minutes.

When my cousin Mimma comes to visit she always brings me two things I crave from Sicily – prickly pears and wild oregano from the volcanic slopes of Etna. The delicious and colourful fruit can range from the deepest dark reds to burnt sienna and orange but you can't tell the colour until they are peeled. They are great fun to eat and I adore them.

The oregano goes straight into the pantry. It's the most intensely-perfumed and flavourful I have encountered and the difference in taste between this and a generic supermarket jar is very obvious. If you find yourself holidaying in Italy or Sicily, be sure to grab some. You won't regret it.

This dish requires 6oz of fish and a couple of pomodorini (cherry tomatoes) or so per person. Put your plates to warm then lay the fish in a sauté pan with salt and ground black pepper. Add two halved cherry tomatoes per portion, and pour a tablespoon each of olive oil and dry white wine over each fillet. Season with finely-sliced garlic (a medium clove for four fillets will do), some washed capers (five per person), soft black olives and chopped flat leaf parsley. Oh, and don't forget a pinch of the oregano.

Cover with a lid and gently simmer until the fish is cooked. Place the fish on a hot plate to keep warm while you turn up the heat to reduce and intensify the juices before dressing the fish.

This is so simple and works with a few good ingredients. The quality of the fish, olive oil, tomatoes and oregano make all the difference. It is also good as a salad, eaten at room temperature with good bread for dipping into the amazing juices it produces.

John with Zia Pina and mum
at his christening in 1960

{ england calling }

2

Sir,

    With reference to your letter of 4th January, 1959, I am directed by the Secretary of State to say that as Mr. Salvatore Dammone's permitted stay in this country does not expire until 9th May, 1959, it is regretted that no further extension of his stay can be granted at present. His passport and Police Registration Certificate are, therefore, returned herewith and should be resubmitted through the British Hotels and Restaurants Association nearer to the date of expiry of his permitted stay in this country.

    I am to add that it is noted from the records of this Department that Mr. Dammone's wife arrived in this country on 29th November, 1958, for two months. The Secretary of State would be grateful, therefore, if Mrs. Dammone could be instructed to forward her passport and Police Registration Certificate to this Department so that her stay in this country may be brought into line with her husband's stay.

    I am, Sir,
    Your obedient Servant,

M. G. Jeremiah.

The Manager,
The Parkway Hotel (Leeds) Ltd.,
Leeds. 16.

It is hard to imagine how strange England must have seemed to the newlywed Dammones.

The language was incomprehensible, the weather miserable and the food devoid of taste. But it was the place that offered work opportunities.

They couldn't do much about the weather, but set about the other challenges with gusto. Their English improved rapidly and before long they would be introducing the Brits to new eating experiences, in, of all places, their own transport café.

But along the way, there were other, everyday learning experiences in their adopted country.

An elderly resident of Leeds once recounted to us how a certain foreign couple who became her neighbours in a traditional working class area soon made their presence felt. With no electricity and only candles for light, Salvo set about the task of warming up the place.

His efforts to light a fire were a little over-enthusiastic and resulted in the fire brigade being summoned. Similarly, he struggled to come to terms with the English custom of Bonfire Night. Impatient as ever to ignite his bonfire, he decided a good dose of petrol was called for. This particular learning experience certainly went with a bang.

GIP: There was also an additional responsibility to conjure with. I arrived on 19th June 1955.

The family, already firmly established in Leeds, was growing. Our Auntie Pina – my mother's sister – came over next, closely followed by my Uncle Pinu, but only after my father had managed to find him a job, such were the strict regulations on work permits.

As it turned out, every pair of hands was going to be needed. The Dammones were about to make their debut in the food business.

> *The language was incomprehensible, the weather miserable and the food devoid of taste. But it was the place that offered work.*

made the 3th
ue Huddersfield (called the Vendo
re Dammone of IIO Town Street Stanningley in the
ds(Called the Purchaser) of the other part WHEREBY
ed as follows:-
will sell and the Purchaser will purchase the shar
ess of Gino's C   Bar, carried on at 260 Kirksta
s at the   cash   an
at the rat
l of the sa
said premi
ndor will
se the ben
ilippo COR
share of
Vendor wil
d business
ker -Charle

I CINO GUISEPPE of 94 York Avenue Hudde
HEREBY AGREE to sell my share in the bu
Bar, carried on at 260 Kirkstall Road Le
of 110 Town Street Stanningly Leeds at th
as to £900 cash and the balance at the r
This Agreement is subject to a formal ag
by my solicitors.

Hire Purchase --
furniture and electric
4. The Vendor will so f
the benefit of such Hire
5. The Vendor will take
Purchaser of any Licence
so that the business can
as heretofore
6. The Vendor will assi
have of the said premise
the said premises for t
7. The Vendor will dis
up to the date of this
8. The costs in connec
AS WITNESS the hands of

Paid CASH £800

3
{ café society }

Partial document (top left):

field, Cafe Proprietor
ess of Ginos Coffee
to SALVO DAMMONE
rice of £1200 payable
of £10 per week.
ment being drawn up

Central letter:

Telephone
TERMINUS 8822
Ext. 66
S.66/1

ST. PANCRAS CHAMBERS
LONDON, N.W.1

26th September, 1962

Mrs. S. Dammone,
9, Stoney Rock Road,
LEEDS 9.

Dear Madam,

Thank you for your letter dated 24th September.

In order that further consideration may be given to your request for employment for your brother-in-law, will you please ask him to complete the enclosed form and return it to me, together with original or photostat copies of references covering his experience as a Waiter for a period of at least five years, and his photograph attached thereto.

Yours faithfully,

for A.G.B. KELLEY
OFFICER FOR PERSONNEL

Encl.

Right side document:

Mr. G. Davidson
- to -
Mr. S. Dammone

A G R E E M E N T

for the sale and purchase of
a business of a café carried
on at 110 Town Street Stanningley
in the City of Leeds.

Lower left fragments:

nuary 1965

the sum of

a/c g purchase

subject to

sworth + Foster

uipment

he is able to do so transfer

ase Agreements

ecessary steps to procure t

onnection with the said bus

rried on by the Purchaser as a going concern

the Purchaser the benefit of any tenancy he may

will use his best endeavours to obtain a Lease of

haser from the Landlord

all debts incurred in respect of the said business

ith this Agreement shall be paid by the Purchaser

arties hereto

It was by then the early sixties. There are two things that stick in the memory from that time. One is The Beatles. The other is chips – ever-present mountains of them, served as steak and chips, bacon and chips, full English breakfast in the morning. Or at least, a full English as interpreted by an Italian.

The family had embarked on its first business venture, a transport café on Stanningley Road.

Looking at Salvo's today, praised in equal measure by Gordon Ramsay and the Good Food Guide, it seems incredible that it can trace its heritage back here, to the place where we all lived, literally over the shop.

Uncle Pinu supervised chip output on an industrial scale, aided by middle brother Lucci, together with a rumbling machine which peeled spuds by the sack in the backyard and another aluminium device for cutting the potatoes – the chipper!

And there was no shortage of customers. The café was next door to a heavy engineering plant, from where the staff would call in for a filling breakfast on their way to work.

Mum and Auntie Pina, on the other hand, introduced a few typically Italian touches. Blending plum tomatoes with a little garlic, salt and pepper on the stove, they'd cook up an authentic and delicious Neapolitan tomato sauce.

As part of what can lay claim to being a kind of sixties bruschetta, this was sent out from the kitchen to the eager customers – on toasted teacakes. We also served what we called 'hamburgers' – they were just mum's meatballs squashed flat!

But the culinary frontiers were about to be pushed back further still. A ripple of excitement greeted the arrival of a new dish on the menu. Steak Pizzaiola. It may have been merely stewing steak braised in Mum's tomato sauce, but at the time it was very new to the clientele. It was on the menu as 'beef grenadine'.

Food at the café was one thing, but we always ate Italian at home.

Getting the authentic ingredients became easier after an enterprising expat started coming around our way in a Commer van that was effectively a mobile deli.

The aroma! It was like nothing on earth. It was a mini salumeria, with the scent of garlic and salami, this at a time when you couldn't buy garlic in the shops.

The man behind it sold Italian products – tinned tomatoes, pasta and other staples. He'd go around the streets where he knew Italians lived and did a roaring trade.

As for the café itself, it was our workplace. We would clean and clear tables during busy times as well as doing the bread and butter.

But after hours it was a kids' paradise. In particular, we were drawn by the pinball machine, a fascination which grew after we found out where the keys were hidden and played endless games for free.

> ***But the culinary frontiers were about to be pushed back further. A ripple of excitement greeted the arrival of a new dish on the menu – Steak Pizzaiola.***

SUGO (BASIC TOMATO SAUCE)

As a family hailing from the south of Italy, we like our tomatoes and naturally prefer the ones from our home region. This is a basic tomato sugo from which many dishes are constructed.

We use tinned San Marzano plum tomatoes, grown in rich volcanic soil around Vesuvius (taking in Salerno, Napoli and Avellino) but you can use a smooth passata or even chopped tomatoes. A good quality tinned tomato will make a good quality sauce. If you have any ripe tomatoes in the bottom of the fridge at home, they can always go into this too. Just quarter and throw them in after frying your base of onion and garlic then add the tinned ones.

We sometimes make a fresh tomato sugo from San Marzano plum tomatoes by peeling first. Just nick the bottom of them and throw into boiling water for a minute or so until you see the skin start to come away from the flesh. Refresh under cold running water and the thick skins of these flavoursome tomatoes come away very easily. This variety has very few seeds and is said to produce the best tomatoes in the world for making sauce for pasta or pizza.

SUGO (CONTINUED)

INGREDIENTS

1 finely-diced small onion, about 100g

3 cloves of garlic, peeled and sliced

An espresso cup of olive oil

2 x 400g tins plum tomatoes (or a bottle of passata which is usually 700g)

5/6 whole basil leaves

1. Starting in a cold pan, fry the onion and garlic gently in the oil till soft for about five minutes.

2. Add the tomatoes, season and bring to the boil before simmering for 30 minutes. I use a potato masher to break the tomatoes down after ten minutes or so. Season to taste.

3. Finally, add the basil.

* As a guide to seasoning, tinned tomatoes will take approx. 10 grams of salt per kilo (so a 400g tin needs approx. four grams). This is easy to remember but when you weigh the salt, pour it into your hand and see how much you use so the next time you can season *all'occhio* as they say, with your eye. Always taste the sugo after seasoning and be careful of reducing too much as this is when things get salty.

eeds weekend starts
n a Thursday for the
wer 18's at the . . . . **Blues Gardenia**

WHITE HORSE STREET (opposite C. & A.

dmission and Membership . . . . FREE!!!

st April   —   **Opening Night**   —   1st Apri

7.30 — 11 p.m.

S & D ENTERPRISES proudly present

Thursday's Children

4

{ house of cards }

JOHN: The Blue Gardenia was one of my father's coffee bar ventures. But it became famous for very different reasons.

On the ground floor there was a café and downstairs was a basement that became a legendary nightclub. Some of the emerging stars of the sixties played there – Joe Cocker and Rod Stewart to name but two.

GIP: I remember going downstairs and seeing a drum kit all set up, so of course I had a little bash around on it. I was too young to take it all in, but years later a promoter told me about the time Joe Cocker played there. He was working night shift on the buses and had to run for his train back to Sheffield to be there in time to go to work.

This didn't leave enough time to deal with payment, so the promoter sent him a postal order.

But there was another side to the Blue Gardenia. Upstairs

A promoter told me about the time Joe Cocker played there. He was working night shift on the buses and had to run for his train back to Sheffield to be there in time to go to work.

was its secret – an illegal gambling den. At the time lots of Italian cafés had card games going on in back rooms.

This particular one had curtaining all around it. When the curtains were drawn back, the inner sanctum was revealed. There were stacks of sealed playing cards and tables covered with green baize, each with a brass letterbox in the centre.

JOHN: There were some serious gamblers. At times the pot could reach up to three or four hundred pounds, which was the cost of a small house in the sixties.

I remember getting into trouble on one occasion when I went in there as a game was in progress. The men were playing Neapolitan cards and drinking heavily, and the air was thick with smoke.

After a while I began to follow roughly how it worked. Then my brief insight into the

Scopa — Neapolitan playing cards

world of gambling came to a sudden and abrupt end.

I tapped my dad on the shoulder and whispered "the man on the right has got two kings". The game ended in pandemonium and I got the telling-off of my life.

The whole thing came to an end soon afterwards. My mother laid down an ultimatum – either the gambling den went or she would.

The threat worked and he sold it on to some other Italians who continued to run the business in the same vein. Ironically, it was raided a few months later and the business closed down.

An old membership card from the Blue Gardenia. This one belonged to Derek 'Tamala' Barnett

Blue Gardenia Private Club and Discotheque

6, White Horse Street, Leeds 1
Tel.: 28324

Please:—
Always carry this card.
Always quote membership number.
Always advise change of address.

MEMBERSHIP CERTIFICATE

GIP: The three constants in my life have always been family, food and music. In the sixties there were companies that placed jukeboxes in coffee bars; they would come in once a fortnight and change the least played four singles with four new ones from the hit parade. After emptying the tanners (sixpence or two-and-a-half 'new' pence now) the premises would get their cut.

As a kid I would make sure I was around when the jukebox guy came around to change the records. He was an Italian known as *Vincenz' o zuzzuso* (grimy Vince in Neapolitan), probably because his fingers were always dirty from the machines and coins. If I was around he would give me the four singles he had taken out and so began my record collection which I still add to.

Dad finally bought the jukebox from Vince and I was tasked with going to Valance's, a big electrical appliance shop in Leeds which also had a record corner. After studying the top 100 hit parade on the wall and listening to records in the listening booth all day, I would choose four. Quite a responsibility for a 14-year-old in 1969.

The Blue Gardenia, the coffee bar dad was involved with in the sixties, also had live music in the basement and my fascination with music started by exploring the basement as a kid while dad did his business, banging a drum kit and letting my imagination wander.

Music has been part of my life ever since and naturally it became part of what we do in business. We have fed James Brown, Roseanne Cash, Robert Plant, Jimmy Smith, Corrine Bailey Rae, Vinissio Caposela and Razorlight to name a few, as well as countless international DJs and electronic artists.

A big thrill for me was a visit to the restaurant by Seymour Stein, vice president of Warner Brothers records but more importantly the boss of Sire Records when he discovered and signed some of the seminal artists of the seventies and eighties.

The Ramones, Madonna, Talking Heads, Undertones, Depeche Mode and The Cure are a fraction of his signings. He wanted eggplant (melanzane) for lunch and declared our aubergines alla Parmigiana the best he had eaten anywhere... except a little place in New York with no name which he promised to take me if I was ever in the Big Apple.

What a charming fella.

MELANZANE —
LA CARNE DEL POPOLO

Aubergines — the meat of the masses. At least, that's what it seemed like in the south of Italy in the early 1970s. Just like the other staples, courgettes or zucchini, it's the creative skill of the cooks that were the magic ingredient.

Long before Heston Blumental started conjuring up odd mixtures in the kitchen, there were all kinds of experiments with this commonplace vegetable. Would you believe a kind of baked layered aubergine and chocolate lasagne or a *sauté al funghetto* but with aubergines instead of mushrooms, and even aubergines stuffed with ice cream.

I find it odd that people coming from such a strong culture of traditionalism are so inventive when it comes to the playful treatment of some ingredients. As a rule though the majority still keep it traditional.

A beautifully fresh mozzarella di bufala ordered in a restaurant may come naked on the plate and even warrant a frown from the waiter should you request oil before you have tasted it. I had an amusing moment in a local bar persuading the barista that my wife would enjoy her espresso without sugar. "But it will be bitter!" he said anxiously, totally secure in the knowledge that the only correct way to enjoy the coffee was his way, with the correct amount of sugar. Sure enough the next coffees he made were presented ready sweetened. The peninsula can be sophisticated, modern and highbrow as you like but small town Italy can still be deeply rooted in old ways .

Italian cuisine, proudly cooking with tradition or shackled by regional culinary pride? You decide.

This recipe is the classic dish my Nonna Francesca put on the table regularly, followed by mum in my teenage years. At one point I couldn't bear to look at those purple shiny things in the pantry and the aversion lasted for a good few years.

In a spooky twist my wife, who learned from my mother, now makes it on a regular basis too. She likes the pale violet to white globe aubergines (beloved of Sicilians everywhere) whereas Nonna liked to use the long thin ones popular in Campania.

Other regions in Italy have different preferences. My veg buyer in Milan market tells me the Romans like the 'tondo' or round ones.

There's no right answer — just go with what's fresh and top quality.

PARMIGIANA DI MELANZANE

This recipe features cooked aubergines layered with mozzarella, tomato sugo and Parmesan then baked as you would a lasagne. It is simple to make with endless variations. You can pan fry, grill, bake or batter and fry the aubergines. Some like to use a meat ragu as the sugo, or bung in any cheese that happens to be handy. Yesterday's leftover arrabiata makes a great layer too.

1. First, make a tomato sugo (see recipe page 40).
2. Whisk together eggs, Pecorino, pepper and salt .You will also need some grated Parmesan (or Pecorino Romano if you prefer) and chopped cow's milk mozzarella.
3. Cut the aubergines into half-centimetre thick slices. Flour and dip into the egg mix — if it's a bit too thick, loosen it with a tablespoon of water or milk.
4. Gently shallow fry on both sides in plenty of veg oil (one-inch deep) and rest on kitchen paper turning the slices to absorb any surplus oil. They will have a nice tasty omelette-like coating.
5. In a deep dish, layer the ingredients. Start with the sauce on bottom, then aubergines, sauce and cheeses and finish with a turn of the pepper grinder. Repeat for three layers and leave out mozzarella on the top layer.
6. Bake at 180°C (gas mark 4) for 40 minutes. Keep your eye on it and turn down to 160°C if necessary. Top with mozzarella on for the last ten minutes.
8. Leave to rest for 20 minutes before eating.

* I have deliberately not put any weights or measures on here, because using basic judgment and adjusting it to your taste will bring the best results. Express yourself!

5

{ **back to the old country** }

Gip at the wheel of dad's Ford
Cortina 1600 E, circa 1974

GIP: I well remember the phone call. I had gone down to Torquay with my best friend and his family. My father had taken the rest of the family to Italy in his Ford Cortina 1600E, complete with posh aerial and racing trim.

Mind you, it wasn't posh for long. After a few encounters with the Italian way of driving, the bodywork was adorned with dents and prangs. My father would brush these off as a mere part of the routine of daily motoring, taking a hammer to the unfortunate Cortina to bash the panels back into place. He was kept busy with these rudimentary repairs.

I remember on one particular occasion driving to Amalfi via the coast road, a journey on which he crashed the car three times.

When I got back from the holiday in Torquay, my mother and brothers had returned from Italy by train, leaving my father in Salerno. The call from him came out of the blue and the message was brief: "Send Gip over".

I was 17 and had just started at Thomas Danby Catering College, but within days I was getting off a plane in Rome, wearing my Crombie, my best white Sta-prest, Royals and red socks, not to mention my vinyl leather-look hat, checked shirt and V-necked jumper with a white rose of Yorkshire emblazoned on it.

My uncle Franco met me at the airport and greeted me, aghast at the sight. "What the ****** are you doing dressed like that?" were his first words.

Then again, it was 1972.

The day got worse when I arrived at the Trattoria dello Sport. It seemed my father had bought the restaurant after getting to know some of the grandees of local business, who I was now standing before.

"This is my son, the chef," said my father by way of introduction. They looked me up and down and must have quickly concluded what I really was – clueless. And so it was that I had my baptism of fire in the restaurant business. I set to work at the Trattoria dello Sport.

The Trattoria dello Sport

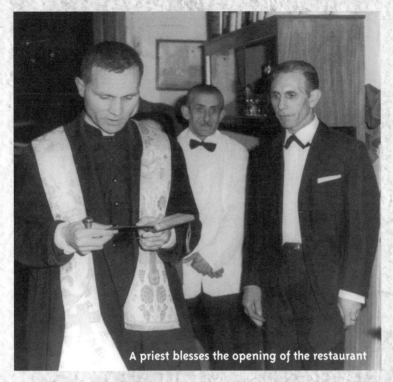

A priest blesses the opening of the restaurant

Zio Luigi working behind the bar

Mum and dad at the I Due Tigli opening

Staff at
I Due Tigli

John's school photo – he's second from left on the back row

JOHN: The rest of the family soon followed, and I found myself at school in Italy. The schools there were open six days a week. You started early at 8.30 and finished at 1.30. I'd do my homework and then in the evening I'd be working at the till in the restaurant. Before long there was yet another restaurant. It was named I Due Tigli after a local landmark, two massive Linden trees joined together. Business was going well, one of the mainstays being weddings, which are often grand and opulent affairs in Italy.

My dad really enjoyed the theatrical aspects of a wedding. Guests would partake of a multi-course meal, and then it would be time for the wedding cake – typically a six-tier creation.

He would turn off the lights and crank up the music. We played Ode to Joy performed by Walter Carlos from the Clockwork Orange soundtrack (it was released on a 45rpm single in Italy).

Then in the darkened room, and to rapturous applause, the waiters marched imperiously in line from the kitchen with the cake illuminated fabulously by flaming silver coupes.

By now Gip, at the age of 18, was running the Trattoria dello Sport, doing everything from the cooking to paying the suppliers.

The mind boggles!

GIP: The Trattoria was a very, very busy restaurant. We'd do something like 250 to 350 pizzas on Saturday and Sunday nights. We'd be working flat out at the stoves, the place would be packed and from the open door of the kitchen there would be a queue snaking outside onto the street waiting for takeaway pizzas. Waiting customers would while away the time queuing by watching us working the ovens and stove tops in the searing heat. That's the kind of environment we were working in.

Outside the work environment, it took some time to adjust to life in Italy. Men dressed totally differently. They had handbags and fitted trousers, and their blow-dried hairstyles were strange to someone brought up on the suedehead and bovver boot look in Leeds.

Something else I found quite alien was the custom of taking a couple of hours sleep in the afternoon. I'd find myself walking around a totally deserted city at these times, with no-one else around.

But my time in Italy was time well-spent. The old proprietor who sold the trattoria to dad had taken a shine to me and would spend time in the afternoons when everyone else had gone for their siesta imparting his wisdom and knowledge about his culinary world. He was a formidable old chap who was a real master of his craft. He taught me all I knew about the art of making pizza and his breadth of knowledge was inspirational. If there was one dish that cemented our reputation in Salerno, this was it.

The produce we used was always fresh and carefully chosen. The food would be prepared in the morning and put in a glass-walled fridge so the customers could see what was on offer.

I recall whole boiled octopus, roasted artichokes, arancini (little risotto balls with creamy butter in the middle), all ready to deep-fry. There were also plates of pork, veal and young goat ready for the chargrill and wood-burning ovens.

And seafood to die for… shiny fresh anchovies, clams, sea bream, mussels and seppioline – baby cuttlefish the size of buttons fried whole and served with salt and lemon.

As well as my mentor in the kitchen, there were other remarkable characters. Foremost among them was a small hunchbacked man called Ninuccio who used to take care of front of house.

A well-known figure in the local community, he was greeted by everyone as "Il cavaliere".

This translates as 'the knight' and is a title bestowed on someone who has worked in the same employ for 25 years. He and I would often walk down the Via Roma, a handsome avenue one road back from the Lungomare seafront and a red-light area from sundown. All the girls knew him, which I found a little strange at the time.

In certain parts of Italy, it's considered good luck to touch a hunchback. He had a great sense of humour and would play on this superstition. He'd spot a woman coming towards him, then just as she was about to reach out to touch him, he'd spin around and shout "seen you!", at which point the blushing woman would scuttle away, leaving him convulsed with laughter.

Perhaps I should have followed the old folk legend and given him a little rub myself because it wasn't long before our luck ran out.

Ninuccio cuts the ribbon at the opening of the new restaurant

A WORD OR TWO ABOUT PASTA...

I love pasta, and so do all my family. A lot. We obsess about it constantly and cook some every day. It is quintessentially Italian, the country's definitive contribution to global cuisine. Easy to cook, it's not easy to understand – but when you do it is elevated from the merely good to the sublime.

Many Italians I know just won't eat pasta in the UK, citing all kinds of reasons. But I find it's mainly because they feel many non-Italians haven't the cultural background or knowledge to prepare it correctly with the respect demanded of it. It's the reason we are always nipping over to Italy with chefs and staff. A few days eating, observing and listening is often enough to 'discover America' as the Neapolitans cheekily put it.

It's actually very simple to make a good dish of pasta as long as the golden rules are followed.

First and foremost, the pasta itself. It needs to be good quality. There really is no excuse to buy the cheapest value brands when the difference it makes to a portion runs into pennies. Don't compromise.

Fresh or dried? People often ask me two questions – what's the difference and which is best? The answer is always the same. The difference is 60-80 hours and the best is the one you prefer. Good quality dried pasta is dried gently after being slowly pushed through bronze dies, whereas low quality brands fly through Teflon dies and are then dried at super speed in giant hair driers that are a few degrees short of baking the pasta. Don't be fooled by that lovely golden colour – there are no eggs in this pasta!

> *There really is no excuse to buy the cheapest value brands when the difference it makes runs into pennies.*

'Fresh' usually denotes egg pasta for filled pasta dishes such as tortellini and ravioli, tagliatelle, pappardelle and special occasion pasta for feast days and holidays. Of course this version can be dried too. To make matters even more confusing, in southern Italy basic flour and water pasta is often made fresh for shapes like cavatelli and orrechiette.

I'm not sure what that soft stuff is in the supermarket but I'm not touching it.

The water in which you cook the pasta could seem a little salty for some tastes, if you're not sure if there is enough salt in the pan there probably isn't. You need about 10 grams for every litre of water. Weigh the salt out and put it into your hand before you season so you know how big the handful is next time without weighing. There is no need for too many weights and measures as instinct is more important than prescribed quantities. And no, you do not require oil in the water.

As to how much pasta to use, it partly depends on how hungry you're feeling. In Italy they generally allow 80-100 grams per person as traditionally pasta is served as a starter. But if it's a stand-alone dish you might need a little more.

For every 125 gram portion you will also need 125 grams of sugo/dressing. Remember balance is important in a pasta dish, so don't overload the ingredients.

Keep it *al dente* so you have a spare minute for the ingredients to bind. And do reserve a cup of the starchy cooking water. This is handy to moisten the pasta a little as it absorbs the dressing.

To judge when spaghetti is *al dente*, take a strand and snap it – there should be a tiny opalescent trace in the centre of the spaghetti. This is *l'anima* – the soul of the pasta.

Finally, remember that pasta comes in all shapes and sizes. But whether they are big packets like giant shells or pennone, or small ones like orzo and tubetti, they always weigh 500 grams and feed four.

The pasta dish we've chosen to feature includes another staple of Italian food, beans. Though enjoyed throughout the country, they are particularly popular in Tuscany. Indeed, Tuscans are often referred to as *mangiafagioli* (bean eaters). They make for a soupy dish and because they are a substantial ingredient, a 500g pack of pasta will feed six to eight.

Pasta e fagioli

PASTA E FAGIOLI

INGREDIENTS

Olive oil, for cooking

2 or 3 garlic cloves, chopped

1 leek (300g), chopped

3 potatoes (500g)

Parmesan rinds (optional)

2/3 litres water

Parsley

3 bay leaves

Stock cubes

500g small pasta – tubetti or spaghetti broken into half-inch pieces work best

2 tins cannellini or Borlotti beans (500g drained weight)

Black pepper

Grated Parmesan or Pecorino

1. Put the kettle on filled with three litres of water.

2. Pour a healthy glug of olive oil into a big thick-bottomed pan with the garlic and cook on a very low heat.

3. Dice and wash the leek while keeping an eye on the garlic, which should be gently softening and filling the kitchen with a sweet perfume. A couple of tablespoons of water will slow down the process if the heat is too high. When the water evaporates, the garlic will start gently frying again.

4. Throw the leek in the pot and turn the heat up a little to soften them and release the flavour.

5. Dice the potatoes – any will do, although we prefer using floury ones as they break up better – while giving the leek an occasional stir for 10 minutes or so.

6. Add the potatoes now along with a couple of litres of hot water, parsley stalks and three fresh bay leaves. Crumble in a couple of chicken or vegetable stock cubes.

7. I save any Parmesan rinds so I can add in a piece at this stage to add subtle depth to the stock.

8. Simmer for 8-10 minutes and check for seasoning. Add a little salt or more stock cube if required.

Short pasta or broken up pieces of spaghetti are ideal for this dish

9. Add the 500g pack of pasta and simmer for five minutes then stir in the two tins of beans along with the juice. If it seems too thick, add some boiling water from the kettle and check the seasoning again. The broth should taste great by now.

10. Simmer for a couple of minutes more till the pasta is just cooked then leave to rest for a few minutes before serving in bowls with a splash of good olive oil, black pepper and grated Parmesan or Pecorino.

11. This makes enough for eight servings and tastes fantastic the following day. When heating up, a splash of boiling water in the pan might be needed if the broth has thickened.

12. This is an ideal way to use up odds and ends of opened bags of pasta. If using spaghetti, break it into small pieces.

I could sum up this recipe in one phrase: pasta + beans + love + Campania = heaven on earth

The beautiful Amalfi coast
in the Bay of Salerno

SPAGHETTI CON LE COZZE

I arrived in Salerno to work in the Trattoria dello Sport in 1972 and something struck me pretty quickly — pasta was as important as religion, mussels were as popular as football and courgettes (zucchini or 'cuccuzzielle') were ever-present.

At lunchtimes, people from nearby offices would eat at the restaurant on a daily basis and order the menu of the day. One of these was the Banco di Napoli offices, about 200 yards away on the Corso Vittorio Emanuele. They always liked a pasta dish to start with, followed by a main course, leaf salad and fruit. These bank employees only had an hour for three courses, a quartino of red, espresso and a couple of cigarettes but the pasta always had to be cooked perfectly al dente. To ensure the pasta was on the table as soon as they were seated we went through a daily routine whereby Tonino, the old waiter, would walk 100 yards down to a corner where he could just see the Corso at the bottom of the street. As soon as the bank staff were spotted, Tonino would wave to Vincenzo, the kitchen porter, who would be stationed outside the restaurant so he could inform the kitchen and the pasta was immediately thrown in to cook.

When buying fresh mussels from the market don't be shy. You need to give them a good sniff and grab a handful. First of all they should feel a bit heavier than they look — if they are nice and fresh they will be mostly closed tight so the liquid is still inside. As they get older and start to open they lose their lovely juice which forms the flavour layer crucial to the dish. If they are mostly open, feel light and have a strong smell don't buy them and make spaghetti aglio e olio instead.

'Pasta, like time, waits for no man'.
— Gip

SPAGHETTI CON LE COZZE (CONTINUED)

SERVES 4

INGREDIENTS

40-50 fresh live mussels in shell

4 cloves of garlic, finely sliced

1 red chilli chopped (optional but recommended)

50ml olive oil

10 cherry tomatoes

A big bunch of flat leaved parsley, roughly chopped

5 litres of water in a pan with 50g salt

500g spaghetti

A word about the ingredients – it is a very simple dish but done properly with good ingredients it is ambrosia of the Gods so good pasta, good tomatoes, fresh mussels, parsley and good olive oil are paramount.

1. You'll want about 10-12 mussels per person. Give them a good scrub in lots of cold water and if there is a little beard poking out pull it out down towards the pointed end of the mussel.

2. Place in a pan with a lid and put on a fierce heat, shaking the pan until the mussels open. Take the lid off and drain the mussels in a sieve/tea strainer, reserving the juices.

3. Slice the garlic (and a chilli pepper if you like) and put in a frying pan with a healthy glug of olive oil, apply heat slowly and bring to a gentle sauté. When the garlic has released its aroma after a few minutes, add the halved pomodorini (cherry tomatoes) and sauté for another minute, then turn up the heat and pour in the mussel juice and simmer to make a little pasta dressing.

4. Throw the parsley in with the mussels. If you like you can take some of the mussels out of the shells and leave some whole as garnish. Take the pan off the heat.

5. Cook and drain the spaghetti, throwing it back into the same pan. Reserve a cup of the starch water. Pour the sauce into the pasta and gently mix. Because the pasta is nicely al dente you have time for the pasta, mussels and other ingredients to '*innamorarsi*', to fall in love with each other in the pan without overcooking.

6. You may initially feel that there is not enough dressing for the pasta as there is not a panful of sauce – don't fret as it is about pasta and flavour. You may want to dress with a little more olive oil and a spoonful or so of the reserved starch water. Imagine you are dressing, say, a salad or buttering your sprouts.

7. Serve in warmed bowls immediately.

INSALATA DI POLPO E PATATE

Italians in the south love cephalopods in all their inky glory; octopus, cuttlefish, moscardini and totani are all eaten in great quantities. The small baby cuttlefish are even eaten raw dressed with olive oil. This recipe uses the classic combination of octopus and waxy potatoes combined with briny samphire. If you can't get hold of samphire, the dish still works perfectly well without it.

INGREDIENTS

1kg octopus – buy the large frozen ones as the freezing process helps tenderise them

600g waxy potatoes – Jersey royals and Charlotte both work well

3 tablespoons extra virgin olive oil

3 garlic cloves

Bunch of flat leaf parsley with stalks

1 bay leaf

Half an espresso cup of white wine vinegar

100g or so of fresh samphire (optional)

Lemon, to serve (optional)

1. Place the potatoes in a pan of cold salted water and bring to the boil. Cook until tender. Drain and cool on a tray. Peel and cut into 2cm cubes, or slices if the spuds are small.

2. Pick through the samphire, stripping the fleshy succulent leaves from the stalks (though most of it will be picked off anyway if you bought it from your fishmonger). Wash and drain then blanch by plunging into boiling water and cooking for one minute. Drain and refresh in cold water.

3. Give the defrosted octopus a good wash in cold water – don't worry, it won't bite. Place in a heavy-bottomed pan and throw in the stalks from the parsley, vinegar, a mug of water and three tablespoons of olive oil.

4. Put back on the heat. When the pan is hot, turn the heat down, and cover with a lid. The octopus releases liquid as it cooks and there should be enough to just cover it. Season lightly as sea creatures are already half-seasoned!

5. Stew gently in the juices until tender (about an hour). To check tenderness, squeeze the thickest part of the biggest tentacle with thumb and forefinger. Your thumb and forefinger should meet easily if it's tender. Alternatively, it should cut very easily with a paring knife.

6. Leave to cool then chop the tentacles and the body into bite-size chunks.

7. In a nice wide bowl mix the potatoes, octopus, whole peeled garlic cloves and samphire (greens are just as good if you can't get hold of any samphire). Dress with good olive oil and roughly chopped flat leaf parsley. Leave them all to meet, greet and fall in love with each other for an hour at room temperature, gently mixing occasionally. If some of the ingredients are still warm the flavours will intensify too. Take the garlic cloves out before serving.

8. Check for salt and acidity. Other than a little vinegar when cooking the octopus, we don't add any more acidity to the dish. You can however lightly pickle the samphire in wine vinegar after blanching. But remember, there are no hard and fast rules and if you want a squirt of lemon to cut through the rich flavour of the octopus, go for it – it's all good!

Insalata di
polpo e patate

ORATA ALLA PUGLIESE

This typical dish of sea bream and potatoes utilises the bounty of Puglia. In a recurring theme of the peninsula's culinary heritage, the main ingredients are aromatised with oil, parsley, garlic and pecorino – ewe's milk cheese.

The original dish uses a whole large fish that has been descaled and gutted then seasoned inside and out. A dish is lined with sliced potatoes (a quarter of an inch or so) and they are seasoned with salt, pepper, chopped garlic and parsley, half of the pecorino cheese and two or three tablespoons of good olive oil. After placing the fish on top it is covered with another layer of potatoes finished in the same way as the first layer. Half a glass of white wine in the bottom gives a bit of steam off to help with moisture.

INGREDIENTS
1kg bream (skinned, filleted and pin boned)
1.5kg potatoes (you won't go wrong with Charlottes), peeled and sliced into quarter-inch pieces
A big bunch of flat leaf parsley, chopped
3 garlic cloves, chopped
200g Pecorino Romano
Extra virgin olive oil
1/2 glass dry white wine

1. Pre-heat the oven to 180°C (gas mark 4).
2. We modify the original recipe by filleting and skinning the fish first, but your fishmonger will be happy to fillet and pin bone it for you.
3. Because the fish is boned and filleted it cooks far more quickly, so par-boil the potatoes for ten minutes in their skins. They will still be firm and half-cooked. When they have cooled enough, peel and slice (about a quarter-inch thickness).
4. Using 1.5kg potatoes to 1kg of fish fillets would make a large tray. The Pecorino adds a bit of piquant balance to the spuds and the tray will be enough to feed a dozen people. Layer the ingredients as in the original dish and cook for 30 minutes.

POLPETTE DI MAMMA NUNZIA

"One meatball, one meatball, well, ya gets no bread with one meatball."

So goes the bluesy tinpan alley lament sung by Josh White in the 1940s. During a lifetime of eating mum's polpette (meatballs Italian style) this line of the song has always stuck with me because you never needed bread with mum's meatballs.

The truth is that the amount of bread mum put into her meatballs depended on how much meat she had to spare. But somehow they always tasted amazing, whatever the proportions she used. Irrespective of what was available, the maximum meat content would be just over half the total. The stale bread soaked in fresh eggs with lots of grated Pecorino cheese, salt, pepper, parsley and minced garlic could be rolled and shallow fried and would be tasty and moreish before any meat was added at all. Depending on her mood, she might chop and saute an onion until soft and throw that into the mix.

Continued on the next page

POLPETTE DI MAMMA NUNZIA (CONTINUED)

When I prepare meatballs now I make the bread mixture like mum did then add about 60 per cent minced meat. I like pork for lighter-flavoured polpette but am not averse to blending frying chorizo or fiery Calabrian n'duja to the mix. Have a root around in the fridge as you may want to use up that little lump of feta/cheddar or boiled ham/prosciutto. Season the meat separately from the bread mix before mixing together. Leave in the fridge to firm up for half an hour before cooking. If the mixture is a bit wet, roll in flour before frying and don't put as much egg in next time.

The bread content keeps the meatballs soft, moist and perfect for braising. Brown the polpette in batches, then use the same pan to prepare a tomato sugo (see recipe page 38). Bring to the boil, add the browned meatballs and simmer very gently for 40 minutes in the partly-covered pan.

At family meals, mum would cook up some pasta and dress it with the sugo as a starter. The meatballs would follow with some beans or veg as the main course. I suppose it's a bit like us Tykes having the Yorkshire pudding before the roast on Sunday.

GNOCCHI ALLA SORRENTINA

This traditional dish from the Campania region is always a favourite, especially when kids are around the dinner table. As usual, the ingredients make the dish. Gnocchi are little potato dumplings that my son Salvo loves to make and eat since he went to work in Giorgio Locatelli's kitchen just as he turned 18. I think he made a lot in those three weeks! We bake these in the oven so you will need an ovenproof dish.

INGREDIENTS
600g tomato sugo (see recipe on page 40)
60g Parmesan, grated
150g mozzarella, diced

FOR THE GNOCCHI:
1kg potatoes (avoid waxy ones – Desiree are a good option)
300g plain flour (Italian '00' if possible)
1 free range egg

1. Boil the potatoes (start in salted cold water) in their skins until tender. When cooked, leave to drain and dry out. When they are cool enough, peel them.

2. Pass the potatoes through a food ricer into a bowl while still warm, then fold in flour (300g) and the egg. Do not mix too aggressively as you do not want to start stretching the gluten in the flour which will make the gnocchi heavy. A common mistake is to have the mix too soft, so keep adding the flour until it's as firm as short pastry or, if you're a kid, a ball of Play-doh.

3. Knead the flour into the dough a little at a time. The mixture should be pliable but stiff. Remember you will be boiling the gnocchi and if the dough is too soft they will turn sludgy and wet.

4. Flour the dough and cover with a clean tea towel and leave to rest for ten minutes.

Continued on the next page...

5. Cutting off a piece off at a time, roll into a long rods with a 2-3cm diameter – like a roll of pound coins). Now slice the rod into medallions about 2cm long, lightly dusting with flour to stop sticking.

6. Place a regular table fork with the points down on the table. Take one gnocco and, pressing very gently with two fingers, roll it down the fork to curl it ever so slightly and put ridges on it. Repeat.

7. Rest the finished gnocchi for 15 minutes then boil in salted water for five minutes or so until they float. Drain and add to the heated sauce. Gently stir.

8. Add grated Parmesan and place in an ovenproof dish. Top with mozzarella and Parmesan and bake in a very hot oven (set to its highest temperature) for ten minutes to gratinate.

SOME GNOCCHI POINTERS

Gnocchi can be made in advance and served later. Simply boil them and cool on a tray before refrigerating in a covered container. Reheat gently in the sugo when required.

It is also possible to freeze them before cooking. Place on a tray before bagging them up to avoid them freezing in a clump. Defrost on a flat tray before cooking.

I've chosen a recipe for baked gnocchi, but they're also great tossed in the sugo. When the sauce has covered them, add the diced mozzarella and serve in warm dishes sprinkled with the grated Parmesan. By the time it reaches the table, the mozzarella will be just warm enough to enjoy at its best.

These potato and flour dumplings have many variations depending on the regions. Some are made with semolina flour, making them a lot firmer. Others are much larger and have ricotta blended into the dough, after which they are shallow fried. For a colourful alternative, add beetroot to the potato and serve with a creamy sauce of gorgonzola topped with shiny black sesame seeds.

6

{ the return }

PASSAPORTO

GIP: They say bad news comes in threes.

And that's exactly what happened next.

My mother had been unhappy for some time. She had become used to life in England and didn't cope well with the move to Italy.

Then in 1973 nature took a hand in our fate in the shape of a cholera outbreak. It was traced back to mussels contaminated by polluted water in Naples. But the effects were felt far more widely.

It was a devastating blow to the restaurant industry. The health scare, particularly in coastal towns like Salerno, led to a collapse in business from which many never recovered.

The last straw came in the shape of my call to arms. Just before my 18th birthday there arrived call-up papers informing me it was time to present myself for national service. Disregarding my father's advice to simply ignore them, I turned up at the local barracks, joining one of the long queues to the police marshal's desk. When my turn came, I spoke to him in English. This was clearly too much for the poor man. Waving his arms in the air, he loudly lamented his bad luck.

"I don't believe it, I get them all – the gays, the foreigners, the cripples..." . He shouted for a translator.

This was clearly not the life for me. I rang a pal in Headingley and asked if I could stay with him. Then it was into dad's car and back to England, with him taking on the journey in one go.

Having got off the ferry in Dover, he tried to do the rest of the journey to Leeds. Overcome by tiredness, he veered off the motorway under a bridge, where both of us quickly fell asleep. We were woken by the police. It cost us a fine for stopping on a motorway, but we were back in England, and a new start was in prospect.

> *Just before my 18th birthday there arrived call-up papers informing me it was time to present myself for national service*

JOHN: It wasn't long before the rest of the family joined father and son back in Leeds. But even before they arrived, my father was already busy planning to open a business.

In keeping with the old saying about clouds and silver linings, one thing at least was working in our favour. This was a time when trattorias and pizzerias were just beginning to capture the public imagination in the north. Salvo had a lot of experience in the business and the support of Gip, who was by then a veteran of the hospitality business at the age of 19.

GIP: Dad and I went to see one of his card-playing friends, Giovanni, whose son Oliviero was opening a restaurant in the city centre. I walked into the best-looking restaurant I had ever seen; it was very modern, like something out of a movie. Giovanni almost kissed dad.

'You had a pizzeria in Italy didn't you? I had a pizza chef over from Italy for a month and he got homesick a week before I'm due to open and went home. Unbelievable!' So my father set to work to help out Giovanni and Bibi's restaurant finally opened its doors. Salvo would prepare the pizza dough behind a locked door, with his jacket over the keyhole so no-one could see – that's how exotic pizzas were in the mid-seventies. After endless hours of driving around the city between shifts, we stumbled across a place in Headingley. It seemed to have a lot going for it. Now all that was needed was money.

My dad had little of his own and with the help of relatives in the Italian community and friends he scraped up enough money to buy the restaurant.

The plan nearly faltered at the eleventh hour when one of dad's Italian friends withdrew his earlier promise of assistance. But fortunately dad's long-standing friend Richard Manning stepped in and the deal was back on. We signed on the dotted line to purchase The Brunch Grill.

JOHN: We all lent a hand

> *Salvo would prepare the pizza dough behind a locked door, with his jacket over the keyhole so no-one could see.*

Early days at Salvo's c.1976

ripping the old interior out, throwing the blue formica tables in the skip. Gip designed the front cover of the new menu, provisionally naming the new restaurant Garibaldi's. After some thought, we decided against it because of the association with his favourite biscuits.

In the end we opted for the shortened version of my father's name, Salvatore. And so Salvo's opened for business in August 1976.

We opened the doors and the people started piling in. And they never stopped. We had ten identical tables, all seating four. When diners came in the routine was "table of four? This way please. Table of five or six? We'll squeeze you in. Table of two? You don't mind sharing, do you?" It was Hobson's choice. The diners either shared or we couldn't give them a table.

I soon developed waiting skills, although the after-effects of a busy night would sometimes bite back. I'd often fall asleep at school the next day.

		TOTAL SALES		SALES NET OF VAT
19	8	72	23	66
20	8	109	16	101
21	8	186	26	172
23	8	154	37	
24	8	161	21	

NOW OPEN
THE FINEST PIZZA HOUSE IN LEEDS
SALVO'S PIZZERIA
TAKE A TRIP UP OTLEY ROAD FOR THE QUICKEST WAY BACK TO NAPOLI.

CHOOSE FROM OUR EXTENSIVE MENU AND SAMPLE REAL ITALIAN FOOD AT ITS BEST!

SALVO'S – THE BEST PLACE TO PASTA TIME!

GOOD FOOD - GOOD PRICES
WE ARE OPEN BANK HOLIDAY MONDAY AND TUESDAY
OPEN MONDAY TO SATURDAY 12 —2 p.m.; 6 p.m. —11-30 p.m.

SALVO'S

SALVO'S

115 OTLEY ROAD, HEADINGLEY, LEEDS 6

Telephone : 751885

APPETISERS			
PASTA	2 Francesca	2	00
	Sweets	1	20
EXTRAS			
DRINKS			
		3	20
V.A.T.			26

VAT Registration No.

GOOD FOOD - GOOD PRICES

SALVO'S

A GOOD PLACE TO PASTA TIME
115 OTLEY RD. - LEEDS 6
Tel. 751885

Salvo's

115 Otley Road, Leeds 6   Tel. (0532) 755017

Salvo's
BAR & RESTAURANT..
..OPENING SOON!

salvo's
salvos.co.uk
0113 275 5017
115 Otley Road, Leeds, LS6 3PX
dine@salvos.co.uk

GIP: The concept was totally new to British people. We brought the idea of casual dining back from Italy, the idea that you could go out for a pizza and it wasn't expensive or just for special occasions.

So we saw an explosion of pizzerias that then filtered back down to London again. With the exception of Peter Boizot's Pizza Express, the capital had forsaken pizza for the more lucrative and profitable veal and chicken dishes in high-end restaurants.

The pizza section was taken over by Uncle Pinu and the two of us resumed our double act. We were, after all, the two pizzaiolos back in Salerno. He made the pizzas and I ran the oven. He used to love being here and would have slept on the flour sacks if we let him.

Uncle Pinu had a genuine interest in people – he loved to talk to the customers and could recall not only their favourite dishes but their family details, sometimes months afterwards, and he'd ask after their friends or relatives by name.

> _**Pinu would often sing as he worked in the open pizza kitchen – people still ask today about the singing pizza chef.**_

We would shout across the restaurant to each other arguing over everything, sometimes even having mock arguments – it was all part of the theatre. And Pinu would often sing as he worked in the open pizza kitchen – people still ask today about the singing pizza chef.

We once calculated that Uncle Pinu had baked over a million pizzas in his long career as a pizzaiolo. In fact we named a pizza after him and called it the Millionario. Uncle Pinu passed away some years ago but his daughter, our cousin Giulia, now works in the business with us so the connection remains as strong as ever.

The restaurant was soon going great guns and the customers queued from when we opened to when we closed. We closed at 11.30 in those days but an hour or so before, a member of staff would be sent out to prevent more people joining the queue, otherwise it would have been never-ending.

Salvo's had definitely arrived. And it was here to stay.

Pizza supremo plans swansong

SINGING chef Pinnuccio Falivene has made more than a million pizzas in his career – enough to feed the population of Leeds and Bradford.

The nimble-fingered master of dough has hung up his pizza shovel after 20 years at a leading Italian restaurant in Leeds.

Mr Falivene, 67, started his career 45 years ago in Italy, at a restaurant run by his family.

When the business moved to Leeds he followed and became one of the main attractions at Salvo's restaurant in Otley Road, Headingley, entertaining customers and children by singing at the top of his voice.

Loud

Joint owner John Dammone, Mr Falivene's nephew and son of the late Salvo, said: "When we say he sings we are using the widest sense of the word. He is very loud and sings bursts of songs rather than a whole tune. The customers love him."

Mr Falivene has used the same, unique recipe for his pizza bases for 45 years but declined to reveal his secret.

"My dough is better than bread. People come and wait here for more than an hour to get a table. There is always a good atmosphere. I like to keep the families happy," he said.

● Salvo's has been given a prestigious Henry The Duck Award in the 1996 Egon Ronay Guide "... And Children Come Too", for outstanding family facilities. It was the *Yorkshire Evening Post* Family Restaurant of the Year in 1994.

● **THE SINGING CHEF:** Pinnuccio Falivene at work at Salvo's Restaurant in Headingley, Leeds

Tributes paid to Salvo's singing chef

BY DEBBIE LEIGH

A CHEF fondly known as the singing pizza man for entertaining customers with his operatic outbursts while he worked, has died aged 77.

Giuseppe Falivene, better known as Pinu, is thought to have made more than a million pizzas in a career spanning four decades and became a main attraction at one of Leeds's first Italian restaurants.

Pinu, originally from Salerno, Italy, learned his trade in his home town at a restaurant owned by his late brother-in-law Salvo Dammone.

He finally hung up his pizza shovel in 1996 after working a further 20 years with Salvo in his eponymous eaterie in Headingley.

Until very recently he still called in at nearby Salvo's Cafe and Salumeria every morning for an espresso and to keep an eye on nephews Gip and John Dammone, who took over their father's business.

Character

Pinu died last week at Leeds General Infirmary after a short illness.

John said: "He was one of those characters who would cheer the atmosphere and ambience when he walked into a room.

"Over 10 years have passed since he retired and we still have customers coming in with fond memories of happy tunes with him.

"These original customers now return with their own children and grandchildren."

He returned to his former work place only last year as part of the restaurant's 30th birthday celebration, where he helped prepare his legendary Millionario pizza.

Pinu left Italy in 1962 to follow his sweetheart Giuseppina to England after she moved here to join her sister Nunzia, Salvo's wife.

He leaves his wife, children Giada and Luigi and grandchildren Zaï' and Milles.

His funeral will take ... Immaculate Hear'... gate Road, Lees'

Comment: P

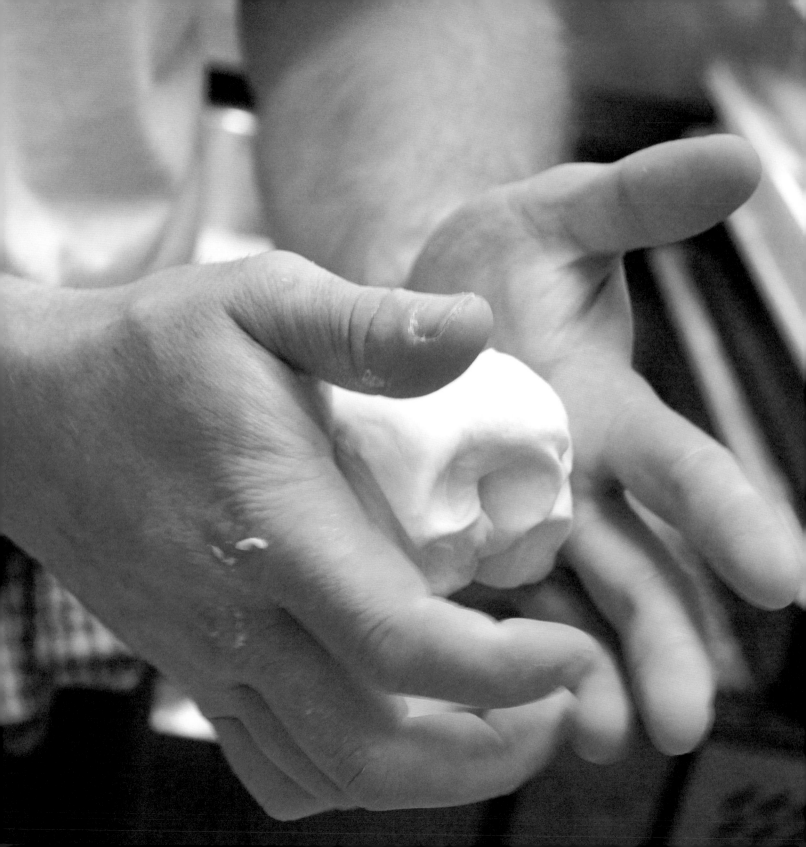

PIZZA CASALINGA

Pizza is one of the world's favourite foods. From Headingley to Helsinki, it needs no further explanation whatever the language.

Little surprise then that there are thousands of versions and modifications to the original flour, yeast, salt and water recipe. But I find this original one the most satisfying.

The best pizza is baked directly on stone and uses simple but good ingredients. Anyone who has eaten a pizza margherita in Campania would agree that magic happens when San Marzano tomatoes, olive oil, mozzarella and basil or oregano in the right quantities are baked at the right temperature by a pizzaiolo of note.

If you do not happen to have an oven that can reach a very high temperature and with a stone floor (preferably volcanic tufo from the Vesuvio area) your homemade pizza will be an approximate version of the real thing. It may even be tasty but the time taken to cook it in a conventional oven means it cannot hit the spot properly.

The recipe and method here is the nearest I get to a proper Neapolitan pizza. It is light,

tender and made to be wolfed down immediately! Once you have made the dough you can knock a pizza out in ten minutes.

You will need a strong North American type flour like Manitoba with a high protein/gluten content and some '00' flour.

The dough is a 24-hour slow fermentation recipe so it is made the day before. This helps develop the flavour and makes the dough easier to manipulate. It freezes well so this recipe will make around eight balls which defrost and are ready to bake in one hour.

You will need some tomato sugo (see recipe on page 38). In Italy we use raw plum tomatoes, either fresh or tinned but not cooked. A thicker sauce is called for here to avoid the base becoming too soggy.

The mozzarella can be cow's milk or bufala and should be well-drained and patted dry.

Set your oven to 275°C or the highest setting. The most important piece of equipment will be a 25cm/10-inch heavy cast iron or Le Creuset pan with a lid. This will be put to work as your hot, fast pizza oven!

MAKES 8 SMALL PIZZAS

INGREDIENTS

450g strong bread flour
(12-14 per cent gluten)

200g '00' flour

400g cold water

20g salt

6g fresh yeast

Olive oil

1. Make the dough like you would bread dough. In a bowl, first dissolve the yeast in the water, add the salt then the flour, half first then the rest. Knead well for 20 minutes until soft and pliable. If you have a food processor it will take a lot less time. It should be pliable but not sticky – add more flour if necessary. Keeping everything cool means the proving process doesn't start too soon as we will rest it before baking.

2. Divide the dough into eight (approx. 130g) and roll into balls. Dust a tray with flour and cover with a tight-fitting lid or clingfilm.

3. Leave in the fridge for 24 hours. Take out the ones you are going to use to get to temperature for an hour and put the rest in the freezer. When they are semi-frozen you can individually wrap them in clingfilm.

4. Next make the pizza. Using the heel of your hand, gently flatten out the dough ball, trying to keep the round shape. Do not fold any part of the dough onto itself. You can use a rolling pin at this stage as we do not need a thick edge for a raised crust. Roll out to 25cm/10 inches.

5. Heat the heavy pan on the stove while you are rolling the pizza out. When it is very hot pour a tablespoon of olive oil into it then carefully lay the base into the pan. It will cover the bottom completely.

6. Put the lid on, turn the heat down and carefully shake the pan around.

Continued on the next page...

For the topping:

16 tablespoons of tomato sugo
(refer to recipe on page 40
320g mozzarella
Olive oil
8 basil leaves

7. The little bit of oil in the pan gives that side of the base a lightly sautéed appearance. When it is flipped over the other side will be fluffy but dry of oil.

8. The base takes just two minutes on each side. Lift the base up on the corner after 30 seconds or so to check it is not burning (Yes, I know a circle doesn't have corners but you get my drift!).

9. Flip the pizza base on to an oven tray and repeat if you are making two.

10. Spread two large tablespoons of the tomato sugo and 40g mozzarella on each. Dress with olive oil and a couple of basil leaves and put into a hot oven at 275 °C for five minutes until the cheese has melted.

11. Eat immediately.

These pizzas are quite thin and, with only 40g cheese and 130g dough, not particularly substantial, but the quantities work for the size of the pan to produce a delicious light supper with a chopped salad. Importantly it is the nearest you'll get to the flavour and you'll get to the flavour and vibe of eating a pizza made in a pizzeria.

Of course you can add other ingredients too but don't be tempted to overload it, as you will be back to eating dough with stuff on top instead of the heavenly marriage you were hoping for. Less is definitely more in this instance so, as usual, the quality of the few ingredients are paramount.

Add whatever you like to enhance your pizza or entice the kids. Chopped garlic and chilli go on all mine along with an anchovy and sometimes a topping of dressed rocket leaves.

Pizza Casalinga

BAKED TRIO OF CANNELLONI

A dish for casual parties and gatherings that is prepared beforehand, sits at temperature magnificently for an hour or so, is easy to serve and eat and tastes blimmin' marvellous.

This dish takes a little time to prepare but the effort is worth it when you are able to relax and enjoy the party with everyone else instead of having to have one eye constantly on the kitchen. It holds its heat well so you can leave it in a warm oven till you are ready.

The cannelloni are layered and baked like a lasagne. You could make just one filling with spinach, meat and ricotta together which would make a delicious dish but having three different fillings is a bit of fun too.

There are about 30 cannelloni in a 500g pack.
You will need a big pan of salted water on the stove to blanch the spinach and the pasta tubes. A good 5 litres will do it. Pre-heat the oven to 180°C (gas mark 4).

INGREDIENTS
For the tomato sugo:
2/3 garlic cloves, sliced
Olive oil for cooking
1 jar tomato passata
4/5 leaves of fresh basil

1. Make a simple sauce with two or three sliced garlic cloves gently fried in olive oil.
2. Add a jar of tomato passata, simmer for 30 minutes and throw in four or five leaves of whole basil. Season.

Continued on the next page...

For the white sauce:

50g onion, finely diced

40g butter

40g plain flour

1 litre milk

Salt and white pepper to season

Pinch of nutmeg

1. Sweat the onion in butter gently for five minutes.

2. Add the plain flour and stir the paste over a low heat for a further five minutes. Allow to cool for a minute then gradually incorporate half a litre of cold milk on the heat, whisking as you go. As it thickens, add the rest of the milk a little at a time. Simmer gently for a few minutes, whisking often.

3. Season with salt and a pinch of white pepper and nutmeg.

For the meat filling:

150g onion, diced

3 garlic cloves, minced or finely chopped

Olive oil for cooking

500g minced pork (beef/veal/ chicken leg all work well alone or in combination)

Salt and black pepper to season

Pinch of marjoram

30g tomato purée

Half a glass of red wine

50g grated Parmesan

Small handful of breadcrumbs

1. Slowly sauté the diced onion with three finely-chopped or minced garlic cloves in a little olive oil until just starting to colour slightly. Add the minced pork, season with salt, black pepper, a pinch of marjoram and the tomato purée.

2. Pour in a half glass of wine, drink the other half. Bring to a simmer then turn down and gently stew with a lid on for one hour. If the pork releases a lot of fat, tip out of the pan now. Leave to cool.

3. When cool add grated Parmesan and a small handful of breadcrumbs, or you can just grate or pull apart a big chunk of stale bread. This is to firm up the filling a little.

4. Check seasoning.

For the ham filling:

100g sliced boiled ham

50g prosciutto

100g Provolone piccante

100g ricotta

50g smoked Scamorza cheese

3 tablespoons cold white sauce

1. Chop up the sliced ham and prosciutto and put into a bowl with the grated Provolone piccante, ricotta and Scamorza.

2. Mix together with three tablespoons of the cold white sauce.

For the spinach filling and pasta:

600g spinach

500g cannelloni pasta tubes – avoid the 'no cooking required before you fill' type. You can of course, make fresh pasta yourself but the durum wheat tubes are firmer and work well baked one on top of the other. One 500g pack makes a big tray to feed eight

50g grated Parmesan

50g diced fior di latte cows' mozzarella or bufala if you prefer

1 egg

1 egg yolk

30g ricotta cheese

1. Cook the spinach in the large pan of boiling water for two minutes without a lid. Take it out of the water with a small sieve or slotted spoon and place in a colander to drain.

2. In the same water you can now put the cannelloni in to blanch for three minutes. The pasta tubes will still be very firm and holding their round shape. Drain and refresh the pasta under cold water. Leave on a tray.

3. Squeeze the moisture from the spinach and chop. Add the grated Parmesan, diced fior di latte cows' mozzarella, an egg and a yolk. Check the seasoning and mix in the ricotta.

Continued on the next page...

Building the dish:

1. Before you start, pour an espresso cup of water into the bottom of a baking tray (one approx. 33x25x10cm will take them all).

2. Use a piping bag without a nozzle to fill the tubes with the three fillings. Remember, the pasta softens as it bakes so don't go stressing about filling the tubes perfectly.

3. Lay the filled cannelloni in the tray. Alternate the different fillings as you build it and if there are spare amounts of filling place it between the layers along with some of the mozzarella you have left.

4. Heat the white sauce and pour over the cannelloni. You may need to loosen it with a spot of milk if it has thickened up a little. It should pour easily and settle between the tubes.

5. Pour half the tomato sugo over and dot the top with more mozzarella. The rest of the tomato sugo can be served separately – I like to spice it up with a sliced chilli or two thrown in.

6. Bake in the oven for one hour, turning the tray around after 30 minutes or so.

7. Rest with a piece of foil and a couple of tea towels over it for 20 minutes before eating. If you are not ready, pop it into the oven, which will still be nice and warm and it will sit happily until you are ready.

8. When cool it can be cut into portions, clingfilmed and frozen.

PASTA ALL'ARRABIATA

This dish has been one of the most popular dishes at Salvo's for over 30 years. We serve it with spicy salami sautéed alongside the garlic and chilli but here is the basic original recipe.

I have not given measures for this as the whole point of these kind of simple pasta dressings is that they are quick, easy and based on personal tastes, a few good ingredients and a little know-how.

Pour a healthy couple of tablespoons of olive oil in the bottom of a thick-bottomed pan with two or three cloves of finely-sliced garlic and a crumbled dried red chilli – or more according to how spicy you want the dish. You can also use fresh chillies if you have them but be aware that some are more fiery than others.

Gently sauté the garlic and chilli on a very low heat. When the garlic is translucent (after five minutes or so) turn the heat up and add plenty of roughly-chopped flat leaf parsley which will turn bright green as it starts to sizzle and spit. After a few seconds, pour in a tin of Italian plum tomatoes and simmer rapidly for ten minutes or so, squashing the tomatoes and reducing the juices to the right consistency.

Be aware that a tin of good quality Italian plum tomatoes (such as San Marzano, grown in Campania, the most sought-after type for pasta sauces) is recommended. A tin of cheap generic under ripe budget toms in pale red water just will not work for this simple dish that just relies on the quality of the basics.

Cook the pasta in salted water (long or short, both work but please don't ruin it by thinking pasta works without salt because it doesn't – end of story). Dress with the sauce and serve immediately.

This dish is often served with Pecorino cheese or simply on its own.

TAGLIATELLE CON POLLO

This easy and delicious dish is a long-standing favourite on the menu at Salvo's since 1976. We have taken it off a few times over the years but, like the penne all'arrabiata, customer power puts it back on every time.

Egg pasta is very easy to make; if you are buying it, tagliatelle, pappardelle or fettuccine will do – they are all long ribbon pastas of varying width. You can buy quality dried egg pasta in good shops – it's superb and cooks in 90 seconds, almost as quickly as freshly-made. The good quality stuff has at least six eggs per kilo. Don't think for one minute that that commercial soft stuff in supermarket chillers is necessarily fresh. It just means it is soft. Check the labels before buying any of that stuff.

I have not put many measurements in the recipe. Use your mind's eye (as well as your mind) to visualise the finished dish and how much you would need to complete it.

INGREDIENTS

300g plain flour
100g semolina rimacinata di grana duro (fine semolina flour)
Pinch of salt
4 eggs
4 mushrooms, sliced

1 tablespoon chopped onion
2 chicken breasts
1 garlic clove, chopped
Butter
Sprig of rosemary
Salt and freshly ground pepper, to season

Cream
Grated Parmesan, to taste

1. Let's say we are making pasta for four people. Allow 100g pasta per person.

2. Start with 300g of plain flour and 100g of fine semolina (*semola rimacinata*) which makes it firmer with a little more 'bite'. Place onto a table top, add a pinch of salt and make a well in the middle. Crack four eggs into the middle and, using a swirling motion, incorporate the eggs into the flour and knead for ten minutes with the heel of your hand until it is smooth and pliable like plasticine or Play-doh. If it feels a little dry, wet your hands and incorporate a little water. Music and a glass of wine improves this stage no end. Wrap in a clean tea towel (or clingfilm) and rest for 20 minutes or so in the fridge.

> Dad told me a story when I passed comment on Italian lotharios: "You think Sicilian men are thinking lascivious things because they stare at women's breasts like that? You're wrong son, firmness of breast denotes experience of pasta making, and they're looking for a good wife who can cook, the rest is a bonus!"
> Or something like that.

4. I reckon four sliced mushrooms and a tablespoon of chopped onion with six thin strips (less than half a breast) of chicken would be plenty for one person with 100g pasta

6. Sauté the onions in a little butter. Stir in a chopped clove of garlic and sliced mushrooms followed by a little more butter and the strips of raw chicken breast. Cook for five minutes. Add a sprig of rosemary and season with salt and freshly-ground pepper. Add cream (three tablespoons per person is enough). Simmer gently, add a pinch of grated Parmesan per person and check the seasoning. Take off the heat.

7. Cook the pasta, reserving a little of the cooking liquid. Drain, add the sauce and stir in some diced cold butter (a small cube, as big as a fruit pastille, per person) to thicken and enrich the sauce. If you want it saucier, stir in a little of the cooking water. More cream would just make it claggy and too creamy and we know three tablespoons per person is plenty. Serve on hot plates with Parmesan.

Tagliatelle con pollo

STUFFED ZUCCHINI FLOWERS

When we lived in Salerno in the early seventies, one of my abiding memories was zucchini... everywhere! Courgettes would be consumed with relish in pasta, with fish or meat, fried, baked, stuffed, pickled, savoury, sweet, hot, cold and lukewarm. I even remember going to a famous ice-cream parlour and tasting courgette ice-cream. They certainly loved their *cuccuzzielle* as they are known in the local dialect.

The flowers too were always eaten, never thrown away. Many times we would come home to find a plate of the flowers, pan-fried in a coating of well-seasoned egg and Pecorino, just sitting there on the table waiting to be eaten as a snack.

The flowers are superb stuffed and served as an aperitivo snack or appetiser with a glass of Prosecco in the garden. They work well too as part of a regional pasta dish with spaghettoni, sauté onions and grated courgettes, well-seasoned and served with Pecorino, finished with a raw egg yolk on top. The flowers are stirred in for the last few minutes of cooking.

In the past I have been cheeky and raided my neighbour's greenhouses in summer as they didn't use the flowers when growing their courgettes. But now they have 'discovered America' as we say in Campania, they too enjoy them.

We are fortunate in

having an excellent source of courgettes in the shape of Bill at Holly Bush farm just down the road from Salvo's in Kirkstall, who supplies us with all the flowers he grows when they come into season.

The male flowers grow first on the plant. After they pollinate the female flowers, they wilt and fall off so they have to be picked just at the right time.

The female flowers are bigger, firmer and stronger. Those available in the supermarket are usually female, and sometimes come with the courgette attached.

If I had to pick a favourite way of serving this delicacy, then it would have to be stuffing them with

mozzarella and anchovies and deep-frying them.

The dish is very simple to make. Just make a little batter by stirring 100g plain flour and 50g cornflour into 250ml of fizzy water (beer or lager also works brilliantly and brings the added bonus that you get to drink the rest of the bottle). A quick whisk with a fork will do. Don't go beating the hell out of it to get a super smooth product.

Drain the mozzarella and pat it dry – allow for 20g mozzarella and half an anchovy fillet per flower. So two 125g balls of mozzarella will easily do 10-12 flowers. Again, quality of ingredients is vital – use the best cheese and anchovies you can lay your hands on.

STUFFED ZUCCHINI FLOWERS (CONTINUED)

INGREDIENTS

10 courgette flowers

250g mozzarella di bufala

5 anchovy fillets

100g plain flour

50g cornflour

250ml sparkling water or beer

1 litre vegetable oil for frying

seasoning and a little extra
virgin olive oil

1. Cut the cheese into 20g batons and pat dry, then season with a little salt, black pepper and extra virgin olive oil.

2. Gently clean the flowers with a damp cloth. Pull the pistil (or stamen if it's female) from the centre and cut the stem off.

3. Prepare a floured surface for dredging right next to your bowl of batter.

4. In a suitably large pan, heat a litre of vegetable oil. Stuff the flowers with a piece of cheese and half an anchovy fillet. Don't overfill them; all that's needed is a small nugget the size of half a thumb. Pop it in and crimp the sides together gently.

5. Dredge the flowers, gently knocking off any excess flour, dip into the batter and fry until crisp and golden. Test first by frying a single flower. If the batter doesn't stick well, stir in another spoonful or two of flour. This makes a light crisp batter. An egg in the mix makes a 'meatier' softer batter which can be flavoured with some grated Parmesan.

6. When cooked, lift out with a slotted spoon and place in a dish lined with absorbent kitchen paper.

7. Serve immediately.

The great thing about these little flowers is their versatility. They can be filled with any kind of cheese, ham, risotto, ricotta and tuna, for example. If they need to be prepared in advance, coat in beaten egg and a mixture of Parmesan and breadcrumbs. Serve with a little dip of your choosing.

PESCHE ARROSTITE

The Italian peach season begins around May and continues right through to September if we are lucky. In the south we have a variety, ll percocio, which we love to slice into a glass of red wine at the beginning of the meal. The idea is that after drinking the wine throughout dinner, the delicious soaked fruit is eaten to finish the meal. Further north you will find white peaches and Prosecco does the trick too. The difficult bit is to not scoff the lot before the antipasto. This is a dessert combining the best of Italy, in the shape of ripe peaches, with a Yorkshire infatuation — crumble. It is simple to prepare, fast, with few ingredients and most importantly, delicious.

INGREDIENTS

4 medium yellow peaches, ripe but firm

120g amaretti biscuits

70g butter, melted

A shot of amaretto di Saronno

A cupful of flaked almonds

A cupful of sugar

Vanilla ice cream

Kitchen paper, greased

1. Make the almond brittle (croccante) by combining a cup of sugar with a couple of tablespoons of water to help dissolve it and cooking on a high heat until it starts to turn a golden colour.

2. Add the almonds and continue to cook until toffee-coloured, then pour onto buttered greaseproof/kitchen paper and leave to cool. Bear in mind the sugar is boiling at 150°C and could cause serious burns so be cautious and do not get distracted or touch until it has cooled.

3. Slice the peaches and place in a baking dish.

4. Crush the amaretti biscuits with a rolling pin and stir in the melted butter and amaretto liqueur to make the crumble.

5. Top the peaches with the crumble and bake at 200°C (gas mark 6) for ten minutes.

6. Serve with vanilla ice cream and the almond croccante.

{ **milking the coconut** }

One of the great things about running the restaurant is that you soon get to know people you might otherwise never have the opportunity of meeting.

So it was one night in early 1985 when I met the proprietor of Coconut Grove in central Leeds. After having dinner with his family in Salvo's, he asked for a private word in the office above the restaurant.

Coconut Grove was a beautiful place which he had built with his bare hands. It looked like a luxury liner, decked out in black and white with flashes of red and a grand piano upstairs.

But it had one fatal flaw. He may have been an entrepreneur but he wasn't a true restaurateur. He opened in winter with hundreds of bookings for Christmas and everything fell apart under the pressure. At one point he

couldn't cope anymore and had to walk out and leave his staff like lambs to the lions. There were a lot of very irate customers who didn't take kindly to having their Christmas party ruined. The whole restaurant – 80 seats upstairs, 60 downstairs – were singing 'why are we waiting?' in unison. It was that bad.

At the meeting he was candid about his plight. If he didn't have a cash injection by the following week he would go bust. He needed a business partner.

My father saw potential. His accountant saw a business proposition that didn't add up. Dad advised the accountant to stick to what he did best.

The deal was done.

We started by changing the whole team, both front of house and kitchen, leaving only one chef from the original brigade. We're still in touch with him today.

The following Christmas saw 800 customers a day coming through the doors for a month without a hitch. By then we had bought out the original owner's interest and started developing the site in earnest.

From cabaret dinners and comedy nights to live bands and opera, we pushed hard to make it happen.

One night Keith Floyd, who then was the first of the new breed TV celebrity chefs, turned up to a live jump jive session and ran up the most wonderful bill for the BBC accounts department. He liked plenty of good food and drink did Mr Floyd!

We started doing live jazz nights featuring international, local and national artists on tour. The Coconut Grove appeared on the BBC several times with the likes of Ronnie Scott, who was a yearly regular, and visits from US artists such as Barney Kessel and Red Rodney cemented its reputation as an important jazz venue.

The music grew in importance and eventually, with a new partner on board, Coconut Grove became the Gallery, a full-blown nightclub until we sold it in 1991. Our music promotion team continued to work in the club as well as around the UK presenting weekly jazz and soul clubs until 2001.

JOHN: That wasn't our only venture outside Salvo's. Before that, we took over an old Leeds landmark, the Park Restaurant, in 1977. It was a beautiful old listed building on the border of Roundhay Park complete with stables and courtyard which Salvo proceeded to transform to his vision. He got this mad artist over from Italy who painted the walls with frescoes of the Bay of Salerno, Naples and Vesuvius.

SALVO'S CAFE & SALUMERIA
Genuine traditional foods from Italy

2005...The Salumeria opens

Later he opened the first gelateria in Leeds, with all the equipment and beautiful continental ice cream parlour furniture brought directly from Italy.

Salvo's on the Park had a huge menu based on the one at I Due Tigli restaurant in Italy. It became immensely popular and within a month the place was bursting at the seams. Gip, who was by then working with a brigade of 11 chefs at the age of 22, stayed in Roundhay while I took over the running of Salvo's.

We also came up with ways of coping with demand, learning as we went along. One was to introduce bigger pans so we could make larger quantities of the base sauces in one go.

Simple but effective.

As well as that, we employed a chef to work through the night doing the mise en place, or

126

food prep, for the next day's service. Unfortunately, after about a year of mad busy trading we had a serious fire in the kitchen. Salvo's on the Park was finally rebuilt but as it was a listed building it took quite a long time. My father was already looking at a new project by then so he and his partners sold up and went their separate ways.

Over the four decades we have been in business we have developed our restaurant slowly but surely. Our first move was in 1981, Dad spotting an opportunity to buy a flat above the adjacent property. He redesigned the restaurant so that the toilets could move upstairs and free up space for an extra three tables. In 1996 we purchased the shop unit next door and expanded into it, creating a bar area and increasing the size of the restaurant by half.

Our next big move was to open the salumeria in 2005 next door but one to Salvo's as a place where you can wander in at any time of the day to have a coffee and a sweet treat, buy some prosciutto and crispy sheet music bread to take home or stop for a light lunch of the day's freshly-prepared dishes.

Over the last ten years the salumeria has gained many regular friends and customers with its no-choice dinners (just to prove we know best!), daily lunch specials and Neapolitan street food. The weekly deliveries of Mediterranean fruit, veg and cheese from the markets in Milan also attract their fair share of fans.

In 2008 we opened a lounge area and Enoteca on the first floor of Salvo's in what used to be office and storage space.

Our most recent move was in 2011 when we acquired the premises next door. After a major refit we now had a restaurant occupying three shop units. It was a far cry from the humble beginnings of the tiny shop unit Salvo Dammone started with back in 1976.

Keeping things in the family we were thrilled when our sister-in-law, an interiors specialist, accepted our invitation to completely update the restaurant with a contemporary new look whilst retaining our much-valued sense of heritage.

With the restaurant now more than double the capacity of the original, it allowed us for the first time to take reservations after 36 years in business. The table-sharing and queueing outside were consigned to the past.

$\overset{o}{\{} \text{ fame } \}$

JOHN: In 1984 we appeared in the Good Food Guide for the first time. It was quite a milestone.

Until then the guide had tended to focus on high-end restaurants and only listed three or four places in Leeds, so we were very pleasantly surprised. Further accolades began to follow.

In the summer of 2009 the phone rang. It was someone from Gordon Ramsay's The F Word television show. We had been shortlisted from 600 Italian entrants in a show aimed at finding the best neighbourhood restaurants in the UK.

That September a film crew arrived on the first of several visits, and we were scrutinised for everything, from food to our business philosophy. They were soon followed by Gordon Ramsay himself. We sat him down and Gip took his order. The place was full and the atmosphere was great.

Afterwards, he pointed at the old photo of mum and dad on the wall. "You know, they would have been proud of you," he said. "You're through to the finals".

You can imagine our reaction, and the nervousness about the challenge to come.

Gip had to cook a series of dishes to be served to a restaurant full of invited guests, including me and Gip's wife Gail. After each course, Gip and the other finalist were scored by the diners. The dishes were served to the table without the diners knowing who had cooked them. But after sampling one of the pasta dishes, it soon dawned on me it wasn't to the standard Gip would cook. Fortunately for us I was right.

I think I screamed out loud when we won. It was a fantastic moment. But we weren't allowed to tell anyone we'd won until the programme was broadcast eight weeks later.

On the night, we all sat down to watch it. When it came to the first ad break the phone started ringing and it never stopped. The website nearly ran out of bandwidth. We were busy before then, but it was crazy after the show went out.

**"We had been shortlisted from 600 Italian entrants in a show aimed at finding the best neighbourhood restaurants in the UK."**

THE GOOD FOOD GUIDE

TORTELLONI WITH SPINACH AND RICOTTA

GIP: When we reached the finals of Gordon Ramsay's show we travelled to London to cook in The F Word kitchens. I've got to say Chris and I felt a little pressure when they gave us one hour to prepare for 50 diners. We knocked out 150 tortelloni in half an hour from scratch before starting preparation for the other two courses. This is the recipe we presented to the show for Salvo's spinach and ricotta tortelloni with tomato butter sauce.

SERVES 4
INGREDIENTS
For the pasta:
200g '00' flour
100g durum wheat semolina flour
3 eggs

For the filling:
80g fresh grated Parmesan
320g fresh spinach leaves
Olive oil
1 clove of garlic
160g ricotta
Freshly grated nutmeg, to taste
Salt and black pepper
1 egg, for the egg wash

1. For the pasta dough, combine three whole eggs with the '00' and semolina flour and knead until silky smooth. The semolina makes the dough firmer so if you like your pasta soft and delicate simply use less.

2. Make the filling by cooking the spinach in a large pan with some olive oil and garlic. When it's wilted, squeeze dry and chop roughly.

3. Add the spinach to a large bowl with the ricotta, grated Parmesan cheese and freshly grated-nutmeg. The filling needs to be well seasoned.

4. To make the tortelloni, cut a manageable piece the size of a lemon, flatten and shape it to a rough rectangle with your palm and pass through the pasta machine four or five times at the widest setting. The pasta should be smooth and pliable.

Continued on the next page...

For the tomato butter sauce:
1 clove garlic, finely sliced
4 fresh plum tomatoes,
peeled, deseeded and diced
100g butter
1 bunch fresh basil, torn
Freshly-ground black pepper
Extra virgin olive oil
Parmesan, freshly grated to
taste

5. Now roll the pasta sheet, narrowing the settings till it is about an eighth of an inch thick (on my rolling machine you'd need setting two).
6. Cut the pasta into two-inch squares and put a small spoonful of the filling in the middle of each one.
7. Brush two edges of the squares with a little egg wash then fold into little filled triangles, ensuring no air remains in them. Pinch the two edges together to make a kind of clergyman's hat.
8. Fresh pasta dries out rather quickly so keep it covered when not working it and finish the tortelloni as quickly as possible.
9. Place them on a surface dusted with semolina and cover with a clean kitchen cloth.

1. For the tomato butter sauce; finely slice the garlic and sauté in a small amount of olive oil. Add tomatoes and gently soften and simmer for just five minutes, retaining the freshness of the tomatoes. Add torn basil leaves.
2. Cook the tortelloni in boiling salted water. They take less than five minutes and will bob up to the surface when ready.
3. Gently drain them and pour in the tomato sauce. Stir in the diced cold butter – this will emulsify the sauce and make it rich and shiny. Season with black pepper and grated Parmesan.
4. When you have made them once you can modify the filling and sauce to your liking.

MAIALE ALL'ACETO CON PEPERONI AGRO DOLCE

When we received the accolade of best neighborhood Italian in the UK on Gordon Ramsay's The F Word, this was one of the dishes that won us the title. One of the things I learned about television is that there are two types of cooking – the easy way or the made-for-the-screen version. Here is a simple way to make a great dish.

SERVES 4-6

INGREDIENTS

For the belly pork:

1kg pork belly, skin on

Sea salt flakes

Crushed black peppercorns

Splash of olive oil

2 large sprigs of thyme

1 large lemon, sliced

3 finely-sliced garlic cloves

3 bay leaves

1. The belly pork is twice cooked so the first part of the recipe needs to be done beforehand.

2. Take the belly pork and rub well with the olive oil, sea salt and pepper. Place the remaining ingredients on the skinless side of the pork, then wrap the whole thing in clingfilm, taking care to seal it well. Take the belly pork and place between two sheets of aluminium foil, folding over the edges to form a tightly-sealed parcel.

3. Place in a deep roasting tray and cover with water from a just-boiled kettle (90°C). Cook in an oven pre-heated to 150°C for approx. three hours till the belly pork is tender. If you press the parcel with your thumb it should feel soft with some give in it.

4. When cooked, remove from water but leave wrapped in clingfilm and press lightly with a weight. You can even prepare this part of the recipe the day before and leave in the fridge overnight.

5. Once pressed, remove from clingfilm and discard the lemon, garlic, thyme and bay leaves.

Continued on the next page...

For the agro dolce peppers:

2 red peppers

Splash of olive oil

2 finely sliced garlic cloves

60g capers

1 small bunch of parsley, finely chopped

4 tablespoons sugar

100ml white wine vinegar

Sea salt

Black pepper

1. Take the red peppers and cut in half lengthways. Remove the seeds, place in a roasting tray and drizzle with olive oil. Roast in an oven pre-heated at 250°C for approx. 15-20 minutes, or until the peppers are tender. Once cooled, peel the pepper and cut into strips. Set aside.

2. In a medium-sized frying pan heat a little oil. Add the sliced garlic and fry over a medium heat for a couple of minutes until softened. Add the capers, parsley and peppers, and fry for a further minute. Add the sugar and vinegar and cook until most of the liquid has evaporated.

3. Season with sea salt and black pepper to taste. Set aside.

4. To finish the belly pork, cut into four or six equal pieces and place skin side down into a hot pan with a little oil. Ensure the pork is moving freely and not stuck to the bottom. Roast skin side down in the oven for 12-15 minutes.

5. Check the meat a couple of times, baste with the oil and any juices in the pan, giving the pan a little shake to ensure the skin hasn't stuck.

6. Once cooked, remove from oven, flip the meat over and season with a little salt.

7. Spoon over the red peppers. Serve with some green veg and your favourite potatoes – I like mash or new potatoes roasted with rosemary and garlic.

FIG & ALMOND TART WITH LEMON MASCARPONE

When we were competing on Gordon Ramsay's The F Word in London we didn't know what kind of dessert we had to prepare until the day before. Our instructions were to make a dessert in front of the television cameras using Gordon's recipe. I have to say the recipe was a doddle and very easy to follow. Here it is.

SERVES 4-6

INGREDIENTS

125g butter

125g icing sugar, plus extra for dusting

2 eggs, beaten

125g ground almonds

25g flour

You also need:

250g puff pastry

1 egg yolk, for glazing

4-5 ripe figs, depending on size

100g mascarpone

1 lemon, zest only

Icing sugar, for dusting

1. Pre-heat the oven to 200°C (gas mark 6).

2. Roll out the puff pastry thinly on a lightly-floured surface until a 2mm thickness. Using a 13cm plate or saucer as a guide, cut out four rounds and place on two large lightly-buttered baking sheets. Prick the pastry all over with a fork to stop it puffing up.

3. Smooth the frangipane over the centre of the pastry, leaving a 2cm border. Egg wash around the outside and dust with icing sugar. Bake in the oven for 4-5 minutes.

4. Slice the figs into quarters and again into eighths (if large). Remove the tart from the oven and arrange the figs on top so that the slices slightly overlap. Dust with a little more icing sugar and bake until the pastry is crisp and golden (approx. eight minutes).

5. Add icing sugar to taste in the mascarpone and grate in the zest of a lemon. Mix thoroughly.

6. Serve the tarts with a spoonful of the lemon mascarpone.

10
{ The Next Generation }

GIP: Meet my son Salvo, who bears the name of his grandfather and of the place that was the realisation of a dream.

People sometimes ask me, where do I see the restaurant going in the future?

My answer is that thanks to some solid training, some know-how passed down over many years and not least, to his utter dedication to the job, I can say what was once said about me;

"This is my son, the chef"

142

Carrying on the tradition — Francesca Dammone and (inset) her grandmother Nunzia

145

Appendix

{ the salvo's sound }

For the record... away from the demands of the restaurant, Gip relaxes with his immense collection of vinyl

Live music and dinner nights in the restaurant have encompassed jump jive, opera, jazz, blues, Latin and soul from the seventies onwards.

In the nineties we had a music office above the restaurant and a small team promoting live bands, jazz and black music clubs around the UK as well as DJs, dancers and record labels. The Dig! family consisted of ourselves, Lubi, Chico and Ez. We also presented numerous radio shows (both pirate and official) for the likes of Jazz FM and Dream. Our restaurant in the city centre housed a nightclub and a live music lounge with artists like Ronnie Scott being filmed live and shown on BBC1 and BBC2.

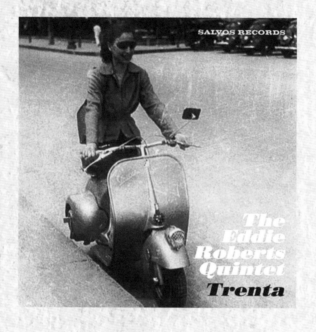

While we were running jazz and soul nights in the nineties, we also released various records and CDs on two labels – Yardbird Suite Records and Cooker Records. In 2006 we decided to celebrate 30 years of Salvo's by releasing a CD, aptly titled Trenta. We called on good friend and ace guitarist Eddie Roberts to write some new jazzy arrangements of some of mum and dad's favourite tunes. Eddie pulled together some great musicians to play on the album, recorded the session in an analogue studio in three days and had it done and dusted by the end of the week.

The album sold out of its initial modest first pressing and was also licenced to a record label in Japan while one of the tracks was remixed and released as a sought-after club track.

Now living in the USA, Eddie plays with some of the funkiest musicians on the planet and he and his band have already released 24 singles and 14 LPs so far.

ABOUT 'TRENTA' — OUR FIRST ALBUM RELEASE

Eddie Roberts first visited Italy in 1997 when his band The Three Deuces played The Bari Jazz Festival as guests of Blue Note recording artist Nicola Conte, along with saxophonist Greg Osby, Rainer Trüby and myself.

His connection with Italy, however, first started literally through the soles of his shoes via the sounds emanating from Salvo's, which seeped through the floor of the Dig! Family Music offices situated above the much lauded Leeds restaurant.

Up through the building's pipe works, Eddie was subjected to a steady diet of Italian music, from Pino Daniele, old Neapolitan laments, Mina and early Celentano, through to Italian jazz sounds from the likes of Quintetto X, Paolo Achenza, Giorgio Azzolini, Marco di Marco, Gerardo Frisina, Nicola Conte, Santucci Scoppa and Napoli Centrale.

His first introduction to Salvo's was in 1990 when he would entertain customers queuing in the evening, then Sunday night gigs with various band line-ups followed with occasional 'Round Midnight' late night Saturday sessions after the restaurant closed.

When I approached Eddie to do arrangements of some of the favourite Italian and Neapolitan tunes from the Salvo's Stereo to celebrate our 30-year anniversary, the result was a wonderful session that manages to grasp the anima, or soul, of the originals delivered in his trademark roughneck style, encompassing jazz, soul, Brasil and funk weaving through the sweet melodies of the peninsula. Pops would have loved it!

I visit Eddie in the States often and, as another food lover, he has taken me to some of the most interesting places I've eaten in. When he returns to Blighty to perform he will bring visiting American musicians to Salvo's. One thing I always notice is how much they love our pasta and find it different to the mainstream US take on pasta.

Trenta

THE YARDBIRD SUITE

An office above the restaurant was our music office. From there we were running up to six club nights a week all over the north of England. Our favourite was our jazz club, held every Saturday in Leeds and, for a while, in Stockton-on-Tees.

The Yardbird Suite was the legendary Leeds live jazz club. When we decided to make our first recording we hired a four-track analogue tape recorder and recorded a gig we put on in Leeds club, the Underground.

Keep On It (live at the Yardbird Suite) was the result. The notes – written here by music scribe, DJ and promoter Lubi Jovanovic – describes this moment in time perfectly:

"The Three Deuces –
Live at the Yardbird Suite"
Sounds like some great 1960s classic jazz album tucked away in your collection doesn't it? Wrong! This is coming at ya' here and now, 1997 style.

It's a cold Saturday night in Leeds, the UK's hippest jazz venue is packed. On-stage, Hammond organ trio The Three Deuces are playing "up-hard" blues-drenched soul jazz.

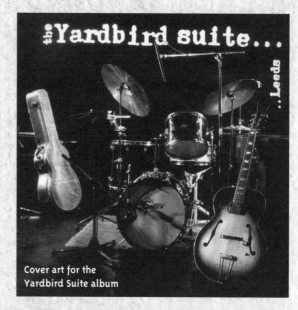

Cover art for the
Yardbird Suite album

Soul legend Terry Callier

Club night poster

THE COOKER

Every Saturday
from August 6
AT THE UNDERGROUND

Eddie Roberts live at Salvo's

Outside, 200 hopefuls queue patiently to get in, being teased by the groovin' sounds of the band on the clubs monitors in the entrance.

No such worries for those inside. A mainly young, sharp crowd (original jazz beards, clubbers, hip hop kids etc) are going nuts – heads nodding, twisting, fingerpoppin', smiling like Jesus loves them.

The Deuces are on form in their spiritual home, relaxed, tight and funky. Brother Ian Rose pushes the Hammond to the limit, Leslie speaker almost exploding!

Young Eddie Roberts plays his Gibson fat body guitar as if the spirit of the incomparable Grant Green flows through him, down his fingers and into his frets. On drums, ex-sixties modernist, Bill White, lays down his no-nonsense grooves, straight for the corner pocket.

Special guests for the recording is ace-percussionist Sam Bell, adding Barretto-like spice to the already cookin' session. Yardbird DJs Chico and Gip stand stage right, grinning like fat rats in

> **_Young Eddie Roberts plays his Gibson fat body guitar as if the spirit of the Grant Green flows through him, down his fingers and into his frets._**

a cheese factory. Unanimous decision – The Deuces are on it tonight.

The music? You know it already. Classic Hammond grooves that respect the US giants ("The Cat" Jimmy Smith, Bro' Jack, Big John, Larry Young etc.) but also acknowledges the great UK organ sound of the sixties (Georgie Fame, Graham Bond Organisations and inevitable Brian Auger). But The Deuces ain't no retro copycat/covers band. Four original tunes plus two rarely heard covers (arranged by the band), and a sledgehammer beat that can rock a clubbin'/dance/hip hop crowd puts them smack back into '97s' cutting edge.

From Edinburgh to London, Three Deuces shows are sold out, house full signs everywhere! A man can go crazy trying to catch them gigs, like the crowds outside the Yard on that cold night. Luckily Yardbird Suite Records has captured that magic spirit and atmosphere of their shows, and now you can too. So put the CD on, position the speakers just right and turn the volume up LOUD! Like the Three Deuces say – "Keep On It".

153

{ index }

ACKNOWLEDGEMENTS

We would like to humbly thank all those, past and present, who have helped, inspired, bullied or encouraged us to write this book.

First, of course, mum, dad and the rest of our family and relatives. Taste is subjective but quality is essential so a big 'abbraccio' to all our Italian relatives who taught us there was nothing wrong with taking a 50km round trip to get some ice cream for our Sunday lunch (the answer when I asked my uncle was – it's the best around, you'd be a fool to have something inferior).

Dad, sorry for laughing when you brought two litres of oil over from Sicily every trip. I know I scoffed and reminded you that can get olive oil here in England. But I was young and daft; I get it now. To Zio Pinnuccio who just had to have the '*farina Americana*' that we used for pizza in Salerno. We eventually got hold of a North American high protein spring flour direct from the manufacturers – no mean feat in the seventies. You were right Zio, it does make a difference.

To all the other aunts, uncles, cousins, friends and strangers who had an opinion, recipe or morsel to share. You taught us that the way to be healthy and content is to attach due importance to food and cooking. Grazie!

To all our wonderful staff over the decades who became part of the Salvo's family; we salute you. Together we built a business that sometimes feels more like a community than a restaurant. There are far too many to list but you should know you remain in our hearts.

A big thank you to head chef Giuseppe Scirrippa who cooked the books for the photos in between running a busy kitchen.

To The Dig! family and all the bands and artists who have enriched our lives playing live in our venues from the sixties to last week and to the worldwide vinyl-loving brotherhood of music lovers we have had the pleasure to break bread with, thanks and keep the faith.

Last but not least, the biggest acknowledgement goes to our friends and customers who have supported us through thick and thin. Your encouragement and scrutiny has enabled us to learn and progress through the years.

Thank you all.

Keeping it in the family...
Gip with Zia Pina